Bilateral Relations in an Uncertain World Context: Canada-U.S. Relations in 1978

A Staff Report

Canadian-American Committee

sponsored by

- C. D. Howe Research Institute (Canada)
- National Planning Association (U.S.A.)

THE CANADIAN-AMERICAN COMMITTEE

The Canadian-American Committee was established in 1957 to study and discuss the broad range of economic factors affecting the relationship between Canada and the United States. Its members are business, labor, agricultural, and professional leaders from the private sector who have direct involvement and experience in relations between the two countries. There is approximately equal membership from both nations, with the objective of obtaining representative views from the major geographic regions and industrial sectors in each. The Committee is sponsored by two non-profit research organizations — the C. D. Howe Research Institute in Canada and the National Planning Association in the United States, described on the inside back cover.

The Committee believes that the maintenance of a cooperative relationship between Canada and the United States is in the best interests of both countries. At the same time, the Committee recognizes that the evolution of the bilateral relationship will produce occasional strains and conflicts. Accordingly, it seeks to encourage greater public understanding of the nature of the issues of bilateral importance and attempts to develop and disseminate ideas for constructive policy responses that are consistent with the national goals of the two countries.

To encourage greater public understanding, the Committee sponsors and publishes objective research studies on various aspects of Canadian-American relations. From time to time the Committee also issues policy statements signed by its members. A partial listing of Committee publications is given on page 102.

The Canadian-American Committee is a unique organization in terms of both its broadly diversified membership from the private sector and its sponsorship of a coordinated publication program combining factual studies and policy-oriented statements on Canadian-American relations. It meets twice a year, once in Canada and once in the United States; these meetings provide an opportunity for members to discuss a wide range of topics with senior government officials, scholars, and other people with a specialized knowledge of the relationship. The work of the Committee is financed by funds contributed from private sources in the two countries. Foundation grants made it possible to initiate the Committee and are an additional source of financing for specific research studies undertaken by the Committee.

Offices on behalf of the Committee are maintained at 2064 Sun Life Building, Montreal, Quebec H3B 2X7, and at 1606 New Hampshire Avenue, N.W., Washington, D.C. 20009. Richard Shaffner, in Montreal, and Sperry Lea, in Washington, are the Directors of Research.

Robert M. MacIntosh   Philip Briggs

Co-Chairmen of the Committee

BILATERAL RELATIONS IN AN UNCERTAIN WORLD CONTEXT: CANADA-U.S. RELATIONS IN 1978

A Staff Report

CANADIAN-AMERICAN COMMITTEE
sponsored by   1496764
C. D. Howe Research Institute (Canada)
National Planning Association (U.S.A.)

Legal Deposit — 4th Quarter 1978
Quebec National Library
Library of Congress Catalogue Number 78-71435
ISBN 0-88806-044-0
November, 1978, $4.00

Quotation with appropriate credit is permissible

C. D. Howe Research Institute (Montreal, Quebec) and
National Planning Association (Washington, D.C.)
Printed in Canada

CONTENTS

FOREWORD

Two years ago the Canadian-American Committee published *A Time of Difficult Transitions: Canada-U.S. Relations in 1976*, the purpose of which was to provide an integrated description of bilateral relations. That report, prepared by the staffs of the Committee's sponsoring organizations, represented an experiment by the Committee in finding a more effective way of communicating its concerns about the overall tone of Canada-U.S. relations and about the role of individual trends and issues in determining that general picture. We have been very pleased with the responses that publication generated and believe it has been successful in contributing to a better understanding of the complexity and importance of the bilateral relationship. The success of the experiment has led to the decision to make publication of such a report every second year a regular feature of the Committee's activities. The present publication is thus the Committee's second biennial report.

As was the case two years ago, this report is exclusively the product of staff members from the C. D. Howe Research Institute and the National Planning Association, the Committee's sponsoring organizations. Committee members provided assistance by reviewing early drafts of the manuscript, but the staff is responsible for the analysis contained in the report. In this foreword, however, the Committee expresses its own views on a number of questions raised in the staff report. The ideas in this foreword emanate from Committee discussions, but they do not necessarily reflect the opinions of all members.

The Committee agrees with the major finding of this staff report that Canada-U.S. relations are significantly better than two years ago, when the first report was published. The main change is that a new spirit of intergovernmental cooperation, typified in particular by early consultation on problems, has replaced what previously had been a tendency toward unilateral action by both countries. In Canada such unilateral action was associated with the desire, and indeed the pressure from a vocal segment of the population, to retain a distinct economic, cultural, and political identity in the face of various perceived threats from a much larger neighbor. In the United States there was a trend toward treating Canada little differently from other countries, thus weakening a long tradition of a "special relationship" between the two countries. In the past two years both countries have had to contend with difficult world problems in the areas of economic performance, energy, and trade, and this has led them increasingly to view themselves as allied against common challenges. The current U.S. approach to foreign economic policy reflects the fact that the world's economic problems are impacting negatively on the United States and that there is, consequently, a

greater need for multilateral, and bilateral, cooperation. Canada, meanwhile, has had to moderate "nationalist" objectives in its economic dealings out of an awareness of its internal problems and policy constraints. In both cases national interests remain predominant, but strategies have been altered to reflect changing perceptions of primary national interests and how best to achieve them. Significant examples of recent cooperation are the negotiation of the agreement to build the Alaska Highway natural gas pipeline, the tariff-cutting offer to Canada made by the United States at the multilateral trade negotiations (MTN), and Canada's provision of emergency supplies of electricity, natural gas, and oil to the United States during the winter of 1977.

During the past two years difficult world problems have caused the focus of attention bilaterally to be mainly on longer-term problems and areas for joint action. The result has been that individual irritants, of which there continue to be quite a number, have not created the tension in the relationship that they might well have produced if long-term concerns had not been such a preoccupation. This situation has provided a valuable lesson for Canada-U.S. relations — that a cooperative attitude on a wide variety of problems over an extended period of time has been the underlying strength of the relationship, and each country should resist the temptation to allow sudden irritants to undermine that strength.

Over the past two years there have emerged three particular developments, described in some detail in the staff report, that we believe are important to highlight.

First, there is the challenge from Quebec to national unity in Canada. The U.S. government has quite properly been careful to avoid actions that might be construed as interfering in a Canadian domestic matter. In the United States, corporations, financial institutions, and private individuals have been similarly reticent in expressing their views on the future of Canadian unity. Nevertheless, there is deep and widespread anxiety there about the resolution of this problem. The uncertainty created by the national unity issue has major implications for the United States in the areas of trade and defence as well as for investment decisions by U.S. businessmen. As long as this uncertainty continues, it will adversely affect the interests and actions of both Canadians and Americans in their relations with each other.

Although the election of the Parti Québécois (PQ) in late 1976 made it very obvious that severe strains exist in the Canadian federation, these have been present for a long time and have not been confined to Quebec. Furthermore, it can be expected that these strains will not be resolved quickly. It is inevitable now that changes will occur; but while the election of the PQ created the possibility that the changes would be achieved only by the breakup of Canada,

as time passes there are indications that the aspirations of Quebec-ers and those in other regions of the country can be accommodated by much less drastic means. One reason for this optimism is that there seems to be a growing interest throughout the country in sort-ing out Canada's constitutional problems.

A second major development has been the encouraging progress made in resolving difficulties that have emerged from changes in energy-sharing arrangements. The announcement of Canada's phasing-out of oil exports to the United States and the fear that a similar policy was imminent in natural gas were major causes of the cool relations that existed two years ago. Part of the problem re-sulted from a misunderstanding in the United States of Canada's motives, but better communication between the two countries re-cently has helped ease this source of friction. In addition, while Canada has been unable to slow down the phasing-out of oil exports, it has tried to be cooperative in assisting affected U.S. markets to adjust to dwindling supplies. One step has been to permit swaps of oil. As far as gas is concerned, it is possible that increased flows of gas from Canada to the United States may be available within sev-eral years as a result of either new gas exports, acceleration of shipments under existing contracts, or gas swaps over time (Cana-dian gas could be replaced by Alaskan gas when it comes on stream through the completed Alaska Highway pipeline). Canada would ap-pear to have some potential to help the United States overcome its short-term oil and gas supply problems without jeopardizing its own domestic energy objectives; to the extent that this is feasible, we en-courage the two countries to seek to extend the cooperation recently established in the energy area by continuing to examine the pos-sibilities for further flows of energy from Canada to the United States.

A third major development is that both countries have become concerned about their respective foreign-trade performances. The United States has a very large merchandise-trade deficit, and Canada has a huge deficit in trade in manufactured goods. Despite these problems and an increasing worldwide sentiment favoring pro-tectionism, the United States and Canada have remained consis-tently in favor of trade liberalization in the current round of the MTN. Discussions have also continued between the two countries with regard to arranging trade concessions at the multilateral level to facilitate bilateral trade. We endorse continued communication between the two countries in an effort to sort out their own, and the world's, trade problems.

In addition to these three specific developments — Canadian na-tional unity, energy sharing, and trade relations — the Committee believes that the mechanisms used to deal with bilateral issues de-serve some consideration. From the recent period certain perceptions can be gained about the process of achieving better relations:

• Linking the solution of an irritant on one side of the border to the solution of an unconnected irritant on the other side is an unpromising approach to resolving bilateral difficulties. One example of this approach described in the staff report is the prescription by some that the Canadian tax provisions regarding foreign advertising expenses be removed in exchange for removal of the U.S. foreign-convention tax regulations. The question of linkages arises because compromise is a natural part of any negotiating process. There is, however, a large difference between, for example, the current maritime-boundary negotiations — where there are some shared and comparable interests at stake, and therefore some room for compromise — and the case cited above, where the interests of one region or economic group are completely divorced from those of the other. The danger in linking unconnected issues is that a stalemate will result, with progress on separate issues being impeded. In order to achieve amicable relations, there is undoubtedly merit in the two countries' exchanging concessions on separate issues, but this does not mean that the concessions should be tied to one another.

• Efforts should be made to reduce discrepancies and anomalies in the statistics that measure bilateral flows by organizing intergovernmental sessions to resolve the problems creating these differences. Such joint groups have in the past attempted to sort out merchandise-trade and auto-trade statistics. This is an important exercise and should be continued so that there will be common ground for discussion of contentious issues and so that the results can be used by the media in the two countries to encourage more informed public opinion.

• As a professional and non-political mechanism for dealing with boundary pollution problems, the International Joint Commission has served a most valuable function over a long period by keeping environmental issues from becoming major sources of bilateral friction and also by helping to resolve these issues. In view of the IJC's success, the governments of the two countries might consider whether similar bodies should be established to which bilateral problems of other kinds could be referred. On the subject of transboundary environmental concerns, the question of long-range transport of air pollutants is one that would appear to require greater study, which should begin immediately.

• Good relations between countries tend to be enhanced by cooperative efforts to solve common problems. Canada and the United States face similar difficulties in such areas as energy and industrial structure, and joint R & D efforts on these problems would undoubtedly be to the benefit of both. The Committee recently released a statement advocating that one specific area where joint R & D would be appropriate is in investigating the nuclear alternatives to the fast-breeder reactor as a future energy source.

The Committee endorses the improved manner in which Canadian and U.S. governmental officials have dealt with both bilateral issues and common problems over the past two years. We would like to note, however, that we believe this has been the result of the conscious efforts of both governments and is not something that can be taken for granted in the future. When two countries are as closely associated with one another as Canada and the United States, potentially serious problems are always just around the corner. We believe it is most important, therefore, that the two governments work to build on the foundation for better relations that has now been established.

R. M. MacIntosh   Philip Briggs
Canadian Co-Chairman   *American Co-Chairman*

August 22, 1978

1

Introduction

Two sovereign countries, pursuing different social and economic objectives, inevitably come into conflict when the policies of one have a negative impact on the other. The degree of tension resulting from such differences, however, is determined not only by the policies that one country or the other objects to, but also by the political or emotional attitudes of the officials seeking to solve the problems. When two nations are as closely tied as Canada and the United States, it is inevitable that conflicts will be numerous, so the need for early and effective communication on joint concerns is especially great.

In the 1974-76 period the process of effective political communication between Canada and the United States on certain issues seemed to be breaking down. The Canadian-American Committee's staff report on Canada-U.S. relations published in 1976 identified serious strains in the relationship as being primarily the result of the policy directions each country was pursuing in response to various domestic and international pressures.[1] As its role in world economic and political arenas evolved, the United States had become less willing to differentiate its policies to give Canada the special considerations it had received in the past. The 1974-76 period represented a continuation of the trend set in 1971, when the U.S. government refused to provide special treatment for Canada after a temporary U.S. import surcharge was imposed and the Domestic International Sales Corporation (DISC) tax legislation was passed. Meanwhile, Canada was directing its policy initiatives toward reducing an apparent vulnerability to the United States and achieving a more distinct identity in economic, cultural, and foreign affairs. Policies designed to establish this course for the Canadian economy included the passage of the Foreign Investment Review Act, an attempt to establish a contractual link with Europe, and policy measures to redirect advertising expenditures by Canadian businesses from U.S. to Canadian television and magazines. Bilateral relations

---

[1] Canadian-American Committee, *A Time of Difficult Transitions: Canada-U.S. Relations in 1976* (Montreal and Washington, 1976).

1

suffered during this period because emphasis on the advantage of close cooperation between the two countries on the part of those officials whose business it was to deal with Canada-U.S. issues would have been in conflict with perceptions of dominant national needs at that time.

The 1976-78 period, in contrast, has been characterized by a different attitude toward Canada-U.S. relations. The number and importance of bilateral differences have not decreased, but their overall impact has been smaller, largely because official communications between the two countries have been far more effective. There has been open recognition that both countries benefit from working together on a number of common difficulties; and where interests conflict, there has been a new willingness to negotiate compromises.

Why the Change?

During the past two years Canada and the United States have been keenly aware of several persistent global problems, particularly those of economic performance and energy supply and price. These problems did not originate during this period, but their stubborn refusal to disappear in the face of considerable effort by the industrialized countries of the world has given them a special significance. It seems that, when confronted by a major external challenge, Canada and the United States tend to pull together for support. When economic conditions are generally good, Canada is more inclined to go its own way, and the United States more inclined to ignore Canada, but when times are difficult, Canada tends to recognize the greater benefits from cooperation with the United States, and the United States tends to be more interested in promoting North American stability. The past two years have seen uncertainty about Canada's political future superimposed upon the economic problems of the two countries. This uncertainty has been greeted by sympathetic, but quiet, understanding of the seriousness of Canada's situation on the part of the United States.

On the basis of these broad themes, six reasons for the improved relations between the two countries can be identified:

• The economic difficulties that both countries faced became a constraint on the earlier pursuit of independent policy directions. For example, the economic costs of Canada's search for a more distinct national identity were given greater weight in the 1976-78 period than previously, thus reducing the attractiveness of this particular goal. The United States, meanwhile, demonstrated its understanding of the profound impact that generalized policies have on Canada and its willingness to make some adjustments to reflect this fact. The economic problems also highlighted the interrelatedness of the Canadian and the U.S. economies — a fact of particular importance to Canada, whose fiscal and monetary policies rest solidly on

assumptions about the prospects for export-led growth, which, in turn, are closely linked to assumptions about the buoyancy of the U.S. economy.

• A better awareness of the world oil situation has impressed on both countries the nature of the various problems they face with regard to energy. The impact of OPEC's policies on the United States, and the resulting reappraisal of domestic supplies and requirements, may have contributed to an increased understanding on the part of the United States of Canada's decision to phase out its oil exports.

• The very large capital requirements needed to develop major new sources of energy have made it clearer that gains are more likely to be reaped by both countries through cooperative efforts. The outstanding example during this period was the negotiating of an agreement to cooperate in the building of the Alaska Highway natural gas pipeline. Canada sought gains in the form of the stimulative effects of pipeline construction, while the United States wanted access to new energy supplies.

• Although the improvements in Canada-U.S. relations predated the November 15, 1976, election of the Parti Québécois in Quebec, this election appears to have reinforced the earlier trend. The U.S. long-term interest in having a stable northern neighbor appears to have led to an effort to minimize the strains on Canada's policy-makers.

• The election of the Parti Québécois has added a new dimension to the political debate in Canada. Concern over Canada as a nation is now focused on the future of Quebec vis-à-vis Canada, and this concern has overshadowed the earlier nationalistic viewpoint, which was defined in terms of Canada's position vis-à-vis the United States.

• Although it is difficult to assess the importance of the personalities of political leaders in contributing to good overall relations, some significance must be attributed to the changes in the presidency from Nixon to Ford to Carter and, in particular, to the good relations that appear to have existed between President Carter and Prime Minister Trudeau. There have been a number of instances when open dialogue about bilateral interests has occurred among leading officials. These include Prime Minister Trudeau's visits to Washington in February, 1977, and to New York in March, 1978; Vice President Mondale's visit to Ottawa and Alberta in January, 1978; and U.S. Ambassador Enders' speeches on several occasions.

This report will explore the specific developments behind these six factors in order to provide an integrated assessment of bilateral relations. The analysis demonstrates that at any time there are a great many tangible events and perceptions at work shaping the mood of Canada-U.S. relations.

The Longer-Term Perspective

While the causes of greater Canada-U.S. cooperation during the 1976-78 period are the result of particular world and domestic circumstances, the outcome has been to make relations between the two countries somewhat similar to what they were prior to 1971. Such fluctuations in relations are to be expected. Before moving into a more detailed discussion of the events of the past two years, therefore, it is perhaps appropriate to set this recent period within the context of the several fundamental underlying features that characterize the relationship in the longer term.[2]

First, Canadians will continue to struggle with the question of how to shape a different and separate future for themselves in the face of pressures that arise naturally from sharing a continent with a much larger country operating under a similar economic system and speaking the language of the majority of Canadians. As part of this struggle, Canada will continue to debate the costs and benefits of policies designed to maintain a separate country with the power to make choices that differ from those of the United States. For some, the immediate costs of differentiating Canada's economy and society are not worth the benefits, while, for others, payment of these costs is a prerequisite to maintaining a separate Canada in the longer run. Although this debate has been overshadowed in recent years by what have been viewed as more immediate concerns, it will surely resurface again.

Second, one of the irritants of the bilateral relationship before and during the 1974-76 period was caused by U.S. policy actions that did not accord "special treatment" to Canada relative to other countries, as the United States questioned the need and justification for giving Canada "special treatment" for which there was no perceived *quid pro quo*. That debate has also been muffled recently, but can be expected to re-emerge.

Finally, it should be pointed out that the nature of the relationship will ultimately be indicated more by its changes than by the elements of underlying stability. Canada-U.S. relations reflect interactions among many governmental and non-governmental bodies as well as among individual citizens of the respective countries. There is a tendency at any point in time to focus on the negotiations and relationships that are proceeding badly while ignoring those

---

[2] While this report is limited to examining the past two years, the Canadian-American Committee is also involved in exploring the longer-range characteristics of the Canada-U.S. relationship. The C. D. Howe Research Institute and the National Planning Association, the CAC's sponsoring organizations, are presently engaged in a Canada-U.S. Prospects series, which consists of major research studies on the economic, sociological, and political dimensions of the bilateral relationship; existing bilateral economic and financial-market linkages; and case studies on the impact of government intervention on the bilateral relationship. The first group of the twenty studies that have been commissioned will be published in late 1978.

that are going well. Yet the International Joint Commission, a formalized mechanism for resolving specific pollution problems, and other more informal negotiating groups have achieved successes even when the overall nature of the bilateral relationship could have been described as tense.

Outline of the Report

The chapters that follow show how the conclusions in this chapter about the tone of Canada-U.S. relations in the period 1976-78 were reached. Chapter 2 describes the international and domestic pressures the two countries have been facing and the policies adopted to deal with these problems. The chapter also provides a background to discussions of recent issues and trends of bilateral significance in the areas of trade, investment, and energy and resources that are covered separately in Chapters 3, 4, and 5, respectively. The range of potential Canada-U.S. issues is almost infinite, and those of some prominence at any time are quite diverse. It has therefore been necessary to be highly selective in the choice of the issues and trends presented. The focus is primarily on the economic aspects of the relationship, with attention divided between the major areas of continuing importance to both countries and issues that have emerged for the first time during the past two years. Finally, Chapter 6 attempts to isolate some features that are appearing on the horizon and may be important in shaping Canada-U.S. relations in the future.

2

The Current Setting*

At any time the tone of Canada-U.S. relations is set by the economic, political, and social environment within the two countries and by conditions in the world as a whole. During the past two years three major, and interrelated, problems have existed that are of great concern throughout the Western industrialized world: the upward shift in the relative cost of energy, along with uncertainty about the adequacy of long-term energy supplies; persistent economic problems — in particular, high rates of inflation and unemployment; and dramatic changes in international trade patterns, including a growing worldwide trend toward protectionism. A fourth factor, in the narrower context of Canada-U.S. relations, is the question of Canadian unity, a problem that has been brought to the forefront by the political situation in Quebec. This chapter examines each of these concerns and the policy responses to them in Canada and the United States, thereby providing a general background to the specific issues examined in the three chapters that follow.

Energy

The Arab oil embargo of 1973 and the subsequent fourfold increase in petroleum prices by OPEC sent a number of shockwaves through the industrialized world that are still being felt:

• First, the oil-price increase was a major cause of the severe worldwide inflation of 1974 and 1975, and most countries continue to combat that inflation even though they have subsequently passed through a cyclical trough that would in the past have been expected to eliminate it. Why the inflation has persisted is a source of some debate. One explanation is that the oil-price increase brought about a structural shift in the economy by creating a basic change in relative price relationships; there have clearly been difficulties in recognizing, and adapting to, this change. In addition, some countries, Canada and the United States among them, prevented the full oil-

---

* This chapter was prepared by Richard Shaffner, a member of the staff of the C. D. Howe Research Institute.

price increase from taking immediate effect. By phasing in the increase, they have substituted continuous but modest inflationary pressure for a sudden large shock.

• Second, the oil embargo alerted importing countries to the potential danger of relying too heavily on foreign sources of supply and encouraged them to develop their own energy resources. The higher price for imported oil reinforced the drive toward self-reliance by making exploitation of previously non-economic domestic sources possible. The initiation of the $2.2 billion Syncrude project to develop the Alberta oil sands is an example of the development of new, high-priced sources. The decision to build the Alaska Highway natural gas pipeline was also influenced by the desire of both Canada and the United States to decrease their dependence on energy imports. Energy-related investment as a share of non-residential investment in Canada increased from about 20 percent in the 1960s to roughly 26 percent in the 1970-76 period, and the Economic Council of Canada predicts it will increase further in the next five years.[1]

• Third, attention was directed toward long-term energy-supply prospects. The most severe supply problem appears to concern oil, which supplied 45 percent of world energy requirements prior to the OPEC price hike. Although there is currently an excess supply of oil in world markets, there is widespread concern that this is a short-run phenomenon. One group that has studied the world's longer-range oil prospects — the Workshop on Alternative Energy Strategies, which included participants from sixteen countries — concluded that "the supply of oil will fail to meet increasing demand before the year 2000, most probably between 1985 and 1995, even if energy prices rise 50 percent above current levels in real terms."[2] Moreover, the role of nuclear power, which has long been considered likely to take up the slack in the energy-supply picture, is now more uncertain. There is concern that uranium-supply constraints may limit expansion of the current generation of fission reactors and that development of the fast-breeder reactor, which is far more fuel-efficient, would subject the world to an enormous nuclear weapon threat because of the huge amounts of plutonium and other weapons-grade materials that would be produced. In April, 1977, President Carter announced the indefinite deferment of U.S. plans to build a commercial fast-breeder reactor and to allow commercial

---

[1] Economic Council of Canada, *Into the 1980s,* Fourteenth Annual Review (Ottawa: Supply and Services Canada, 1977), p. 53.

[2] Workshop on Alternative Energy Strategies, *Energy: Global Prospects 1985-2000,* Carroll L. Wilson, project director (New York: McGraw-Hill, 1977), pp. 3-4. Other recent forecasts, it should be pointed out, are more optimistic, foreseeing no serious shortage until further into the future.

reprocessing and recycling of spent fuel.[3] Other countries, however, are continuing to develop these technologies.

As a result of these developments, energy policy has emerged as an essential component of the overall economic strategy of most countries. The Government of Canada, for example, announced a national energy strategy in 1976, the goal of which is "energy self-reliance" — that is, reducing energy vulnerability by supplying energy requirements from domestic sources "to the greatest extent practicable."[4] The major policy elements of the strategy are to raise the domestic price of oil to the world level by 1980 and to move the price of natural gas to a level that would place it in a competitive relationship with oil; to increase efficiency in the use of energy through various conservation measures; and to encourage increased exploration and development of Canada's energy resources. In addition, some careful assessments of Canadian energy reserves have resulted in decisions to cut back oil exports to the United States and not to allow any new long-term contracts for the export of natural gas. The significance of these developments for the bilateral relationship is examined in Chapter 5.

The United States has taken longer than Canada to specify an overall energy policy. A first attempt was made in 1974 with the introduction of Project Independence, which established a goal of energy independence for the United States by 1980.[5] The main emphasis of Project Independence was on ways to increase domestic supplies of energy, particularly oil. The Energy Policy and Conservation Act of 1975 gave the President the power to increase the price of oil within set annual limits as an incentive for developing high-cost deposits and to encourage use of enhanced recovery techniques. A second major initiative was the National Energy Plan, introduced by President Carter in April, 1977. It emphasized conservation and increasing the use of abundant domestic coal resources in place of relatively scarce oil and gas as ways of reducing U.S. energy vulnerability. Disagreement over provisions for the pricing of oil and gas, however, has been mainly responsible for holding up passage of the National Energy Plan in Congress for over a year.

---

[3] For a review of the nuclear energy debate, see Hugh C. McIntyre, *Uranium, Nuclear Power, and Canada-U.S. Energy Relations* (Montreal and Washington: Canadian-American Committee, 1978).

[4] Energy, Mines and Resources Canada, *An Energy Strategy for Canada: Policies for Self-Reliance* (Ottawa: Supply and Services Canada, 1976).

[5] Federal Energy Administration, *Project Independence: A Summary* (Washington, D.C., 1974). As the FEA report pointed out, however, there were various possible interpretations of what independence meant: "To some, energy independence is a situation in which the United States receives no energy imports, i.e., it produces all of its energy domestically. To others, independence is a situation in which the United States does import to meet some of its energy requirements, but only up to a point of 'acceptable' political and economic vulnerability" (pp. 18-19).

In spite of these efforts to focus attention on energy problems, the impact has undoubtedly been less than that hoped for by policy-makers in both countries. For example, total energy consumption, after falling off sharply in 1974 and 1975, grew by 4.3 percent in the United States and 3.3 percent in Canada in 1977.[6] Moreover, the absence of an accepted overall energy strategy in the United States since 1974 is considered to have been a major source of business uncertainty. The lack of action in providing conservation measures and incentives for increased domestic production of energy resources was undoubtedly a cause of the sharp rise in U.S. net oil imports in 1976-77, a period during which most other industrialized countries were managing to reduce their import-dependence, although a better economic performance in the United States was an important factor, as was the building of stockpiles of oil by the United States.

The importance attributed to uncertainty about energy supplies and prices has also been indicated by the recent emergence of a number of special international study groups and of efforts to coordinate policy responses. The most prominent policy initiative has been the International Energy Program, which was established in November, 1974, and involves sixteen member countries of the International Energy Agency, an independent body within the framework of the Organisation for Economic Co-operation and Development. The goals of the International Energy Program include the establishment of cooperative measures to deal with oil-supply emergencies on both the supply and the demand sides, the development of a system for improving the availability of international oil-market information, the promoting of good relations with oil-exporting countries and other oil-importing countries, and the development of a long-term program to reduce dependence on imported oil. Canada and the United States are participants in the International Energy Program.

The Economy

In the past two years the economies of the Western industrialized countries have managed to achieve growth in real GNP, following the recessions or near-recessions they experienced in 1974 and 1975. It has been a sputtering recovery, however, as problems of idle capacity, slow growth in investment, and slack consumer

---

[6] Growth in energy consumption, it should be pointed out, reflects factors such as overall economic performance and weather as well as the success of conservation programs. By comparison, the average annual growth in energy consumption from 1958 to 1973 in the United States was 4.0 percent (see Council of Economic Advisors, *Annual Report*, 1978 [Washington, D.C.: U.S. Government Printing Office, 1978], p. 181), and from 1960 to 1973 in Canada, 5.6 percent (see Energy, Mines and Resources Canada, *Energy Update*, 1977 [Ottawa: Supply and Services Canada, 1978], p. 5).

demand have persisted. In the OECD countries, growth in real GNP averaged only 3.5 percent in 1977.[7] Meanwhile, the rates of increase in consumer prices, which averaged 8.0 percent in the OECD countries in 1977, and of unemployment, which averaged 5.5 percent, have continued to be unacceptably high.[8]

The economic performance of the United States over the past two years has generally been superior to that of the OECD countries as a group and of Canada specifically. As Chart 1 shows, the U.S. economy made a strong recovery, with growth in real GNP of 6.0 percent in 1976 and 4.9 percent in 1977. These rates were both above the long-term average. Canada, meanwhile, managed growth rates that were below the long-term average, being 4.9 percent and 2.6 percent in 1976 and 1977, respectively.

The high rate of inflation in both countries can still be attributed, to a considerable extent, to increases in the prices of oil and primary commodities, particularly food, that occurred mainly in 1973 and 1974. The effects they had on the costs of producing other goods continue to reverberate through the economic system and to be reflected in price indices. In addition, in late 1976 and early 1977 there was a surge in food prices, caused in part by poor harvests of fruit and vegetables in the southern United States and of coffee in Brazil. Canada and the United States also faced increases in the cost of imported goods because of decreases in the value of their currencies, a point that will be elaborated upon later. The U.S. consumer price index was up 5.8 and 6.5 percent, respectively, in 1976 and 1977; for Canada the increases were 7.5 and 8.0 percent.

The high levels of unemployment in Canada and the United States are at least partly a result of the rapid, and mainly non-cyclical, increases in the size of the labor force in recent years resulting from the large numbers of young people reaching working age and of women opting for entering the job market. In the United States, employment opportunities have been catching up with the demand for jobs, so the unemployment rate has been falling — from 8.5 percent in 1975 to 7.7 percent in 1976 and to 7.0 percent in 1977. In Canada, however, the number of new labor force entrants has been exceeding the number of new jobs. Combined with the slow growth in the Canadian economy, this has resulted in the unemployment rate's rising from 6.9 percent in 1975 to 7.1 percent in 1976 and to 8.1 percent in 1977.

The balance of payments has recently been another major problem area for Canada and the United States. As Table 1 shows, both countries have been experiencing large current-account deficits. The

---

[7] Organisation for Economic Co-operation and Development, *Economic Outlook*, December, 1977 (Paris, 1977), p. 4.

[8] *Ibid.*, p. 5.

12

CHART 1

Economic Indicators, Canada and the United States, 1971-77

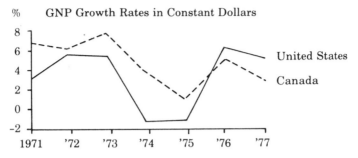

% GNP Growth Rates in Constant Dollars

Sources: U.S. Department of Commerce, *International Economic Indicators,* March, 1978 (Washington, D.C., 1978), p. 37; Statistics Canada, *National Income and Expenditure Accounts* (Ottawa, various issues).

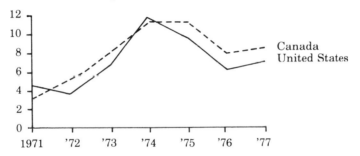

% Rates of Change of Consumer Price Indexes

Sources: U.S. Department of Commerce, *op. cit.,* pp. 21 and 68; Statistics Canada, *Consumer Prices and Price Indexes* (Ottawa, various issues).

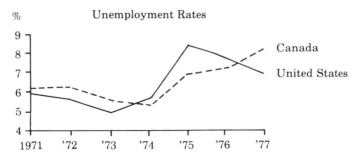

% Unemployment Rates

Sources: U.S. Department of Labor, *News* (Washington, D.C.: Bureau of Labor Statistics, various issues); Statistics Canada, *The Labour Force* (Ottawa, various issues).

TABLE 1

Balance of International Payments, 1974-77

United States
(mil. U.S. $)

	1974	1975	1976	1977
Current account				
Merchandise trade balance	−5,367	9,045	−9,320	−31,241
of which: petroleum and petroleum products	−25,738	−26,031	−33,495	−43,643
manufactured goods	692	1,656	1,039	301
Balance on non-merchandise				
transactions	9,610	7,995	12,550	14,395
of which: travel expenditures[a]	−3,105	−2,552	−2,145	−3,095
interest and dividends[b]	8,744	5,954	9,808	11,935
Balance on current account[c]	−5,028	11,552	−1,427	−20,209
Capital account				
Net capital movements	6,583	−17,212	−8,439	23,202
Changes in official monetary reserves	15,883	16,226	18,747	19,317

[a] Includes transportation receipts.
[b] Investment income, excluding fees and royalties.
[c] Includes net military transactions.

Source: U.S. Department of Commerce, *Survey of Current Business* (Washington, D.C.:
U.S. Government Printing Office, various issues).

Canada
(mil. Can. $)

	1974	1975	1976	1977
Current account				
Merchandise trade balance	1,689	−534	1,089	2,907
of which: mineral fuels	1,277	751	632	−587
end products	−9,125	−10,197	−10,250	−11,097
Balance on service account	−3,765	−4,635	−5,798	−7,517
of which: travel expenditures	−284	−727	−1,191	−1,655
interest and dividends	−1,555	−1,918	−2,491	−3,413
Balance on current account	−1,513	−4,779	−4,187	−4,238
Capital account				
Long-term net capital movements	871	3,848	7,874	4,346
Short-term net capital movements	666	526	−3,165	−1,529
Net capital movements	1,537	4,374	4,709	2,817
Changes in official monetary reserves	24	−405	522	−1,421

Sources: Statistics Canada, *Canadian Balance of International Payments*, Fourth Quarter, 1977, and *Summary of External Trade*, December, 1977 (Ottawa, 1978).

U.S. deficit can be explained by two factors — burgeoning oil imports, which reached $45 billion in 1977, and the fact that import demand generally in the United States has been greater than the demand for U.S. exports because of the strong recovery of the U.S. economy relative to its major trading partners. In Canada's case, the current-account deficit is primarily the result of large deficits on the travel and interest and dividend accounts. The travel deficit largely reflects a sharp increase in travel outside Canada by Canadians; the deficit on the interest and dividend account mainly reflects a buildup of interest liabilities on the extensive borrowing by Canadians on foreign money markets in recent years. Of longer-range concern, however, is a large deficit in end products, which reflects fundamental problems of competitiveness for a number of Canada's manufacturing industries relative to other industrialized countries. The main difficulty as far as Canada's competitive position is concerned has been relatively high labor costs. Unit labor costs in Canada, measured in Canadian dollars, grew at an annual rate of 10.0 percent between 1972 and 1977, compared to a growth rate in the United States, measured in U.S. dollars, of 7.2 percent.[9] If unit labor costs in Canada are measured in U.S. dollars, the growth rate in the 1972-77 period was only 8.5 percent, owing to the depreciation in the value of the Canadian dollar. As Chart 2 shows, however, the rate of growth of unit labor costs in Canada decelerated in 1977 and in the first quarter of 1978, while it increased in the United States, so that the gap has been significantly narrowed. Both Canada and the United States showed more moderate cost increases than other industrial countries in 1976 and 1977.

The large current-account deficits have been a major factor in the fall in the exchange rates of both countries relative to most of their primary trading partners. The U.S. currency declined 5.5 percent in 1977 against the currencies of a group of ten major OECD trading nations weighted according to each country's share of the group's total trade.[10] Foreign-exchange rates are determined both by the actual trade performance of a country and by the perceptions of foreign-exchange traders of the seriousness of a country's problems and the likely responses of government to these problems. In the case of the United States, depreciation of the dollar resulted from both the large trade deficit, especially the oil deficit, and concern that the lack of an overall energy policy might mean a permanent large oil deficit. Canada's exchange rate drop has been far more severe than that of the United States; the Canadian dollar fell 11.4

---

[9] U.S. Department of Commerce, *International Economic Indicators*, June, 1978 (Washington, D.C., 1978), p. 86.

[10] When the currencies of various countries are weighted according to their trade with the United States, depreciation of the U.S. dollar in 1977 was only 2.4 percent ("Annual Report of the Council of Economic Advisors" in *Economic Report of the President* [Washington, D.C.: U.S. Government Printing Office, 1978], p. 111).

CHART 2

**Index of Unit Labor Costs, Canada and the United States,
in U.S. Dollars and National Currency, 1970-78**
(1967 = 100)

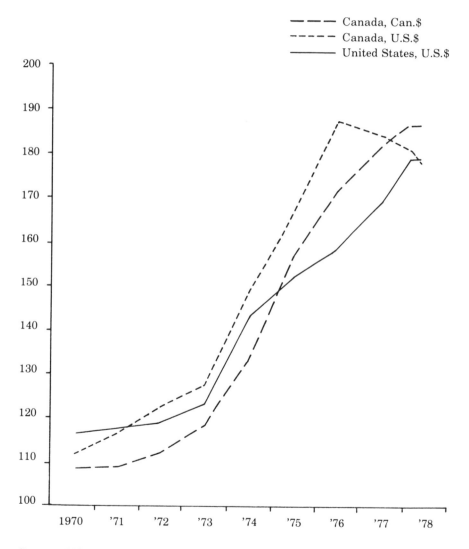

Sources: U.S. Department of Labor, *News, op. cit.*, May 12, 1978, and April 25, 1978.

percent in value against the U.S. dollar between October, 1976, and the end of 1977.[11] Canada's exchange rate has been affected by a decrease in foreign borrowing by Canadian governments at the various levels and by concern about Canada's debt-repayment capacity, about the competitiveness of Canadian industry in world markets, and about the political future of the country.

The application of monetary and fiscal policies, the major tools of economic stabilization, to these recent problems has been based on a philosophy of moving the economy gently back on the desired growth track. The approach has come to be labeled "gradualism," and it represents a contrast to attempts to employ large policy shifts to achieve performance targets fairly quickly. The danger in using such policy shifts is that when one target is emphasized there is greater likelihood that targets that are given less attention will be badly missed, resulting in the need for frequent policy adjustment. However, with a policy of gradualism there is the political risk that an electorate may become impatient with the slowness with which results are realized.

Gradualism has been most evident in the monetary policies that have been adopted in Canada and the United States. Both the Federal Reserve Board and the Bank of Canada have been influenced by the "monetarist" view that the rate of inflation is largely determined by the rate of growth in the money supply. They have tried to keep money-supply growth in line with the rate at which the economy itself is growing by setting target growth rates for the money supply. In accordance with congressional legislation, the Federal Reserve Board has made its money-supply targets public since March, 1975. Targets are provided for three measures of the money supply — M1, M2, and M3 — and may be revised every three months.[12] Target rates for the growth of the Canadian money supply (M1 only) were first announced by the Bank of Canada in November, 1975, and have been revised as deemed appropriate by the Bank.[13] In the United States the narrowly defined money supply, M1, was held to a growth rate of 4.9 percent for the period from mid-1975 to early 1977 and then accelerated to a growth rate of 8.4 percent for the rest of 1977.[14] In Canada, growth in M1 in 1976 was reduced to a rate of

---

[11]*Bank of Canada Review*, February, 1978 (Ottawa, 1978).

[12]M1 is currency and demand deposits; M2 is M1 plus time deposits other than large negotiable certificates of deposit at commercial banks; and M3 is M2 plus deposits at non-bank thrift institutions.

[13]Downward revisions in the Bank of Canada target money-supply growth rates were made in August, 1976, and October, 1977. For a review of monetary policy in Canada, see Thomas J. Courchene, *The Strategy of Gradualism: An Analysis of Bank of Canada Policy from Mid-1975 to Mid-1977* (Montreal: C. D. Howe Research Institute, 1977).

[14]Federal Reserve Bank of St. Louis, *International Economic Conditions*, March 6, 1978, p. 51.

5.8 percent from 13.3 percent in 1975, but in 1977 it was increased again by 10.8 percent, as it had fallen below the target rates.[15]

It is worth noting here that U.S. monetary policy can have implications for Canada. The rise in U.S. interest rates that resulted from the Federal Reserve Board's desire to compensate for the acceleration in the growth of the U.S. money supply during 1977, for example, decreased the spread between U.S. and Canadian interest rates and made it less attractive for U.S. capital to flow to Canada. In order to prevent a decrease in the flow of capital needed to counterbalance its current-account deficit, Canada had to either raise its own interest rates to make the Canadian market as attractive as before or face a deterioration in its exchange rate. Speculation against the Canadian dollar compounded Canada's problems at that time by inducing interest-rate increases, even though higher interest rates were incompatible with the domestic goal of promoting faster economic growth.

With monetary policy oriented to the inflation problem in both countries, fiscal policy was made to carry most of the burden of discretionary adjustments to the pattern of economic growth. In the United States, federal budgets have been cautiously stimulative, with tax cuts in 1976 and some spending increases in 1977 — in particular, under job-creation measures such as the Comprehensive Employment and Training Act and the Public Works Employment Act. The federal budget in Canada has been moderately stimulative since 1976, but overall Canadian fiscal policy has been much less stimulative because of spending restraints at the provincial level and tax increases at the municipal level.[16] Because of the small size of the Canadian economy relative to the United States and because of the large volume of trade between the two countries, U.S. economic performance has a major impact on the Canadian economy. Moreover, since the Canadian economy benefits if U.S. fiscal policy stimulates increased growth, Canadian policy-makers tend to take very carefully into account the fiscal-policy position of the U.S. government in setting their own fiscal stance. In 1976 and 1977 the Canadian government tended to overestimate the spillover effects from the expanding U.S. economy, with the result that growth in Canada was slower than expected.

A major policy consideration affecting Canada has been the Anti-Inflation Program, the system of wage and price controls that was implemented in October, 1975, and relaxed in April, 1978. These controls were intended to provide a cooling-off period in wage demands and price increases and generally to break the "inflationary

---

[15]*Ibid.*, p. 13.

[16]For a fuller discussion of Canada's budget position and of the effects of cyclical movements, see Department of Finance, *Economic Review*, April, 1978 (Ottawa: Supply and Services Canada, 1978), pp. 85-87.

psychology" that became so strong during the 1973-75 period. There are wide differences of opinion about the value of the controls program. For example, although the annual rate of increase in the consumer price index dropped from 10.8 percent in 1975 to 7.5 percent in 1976 (it rose again slightly to 8.0 percent in 1977), it has been argued that this fall in prices probably would have taken place without controls because, partly owing to other government measures, prices were already on their way down when controls were imposed. Moreover, the Anti-Inflation Program had little impact on food prices, which increased only 2.7 percent in 1976 and therefore accounted for most of the drop in the rate of increase in the CPI. The deceleration in food prices in 1976 was an international phenomenon, brought about by generally good harvests and lower grain prices. In addition, because wage increases declined sharply (the growth rate of industrial average weekly wages declined from 14.0 percent in 1975 to 9.7 percent in 1977) relative to the fall in the rate of price increases, organized labor has argued that, in focusing on wages, the program was directed at the wrong source of inflation.

One feature of the controls program was an effort at tripartite consultation, involving representatives from organized labor, management, and government, to develop a more cooperative environment for resolving economic problems. Indications are that the tripartite meetings were not very successful but that some positive results did emerge from meetings between business and labor only. Similar efforts have been going on in the United States with what appears to be a fair degree of success. Meetings between business and labor have been held regularly for several years, and government has been asked to join the discussions from time to time. There seems to be a general feeling in both countries that greater cooperation among these groups would result in an improved overall economic performance from which all groups would ultimately benefit.

Recent economic problems have placed a heavy strain on policy-makers in Canada and the United States, as well as on their counterparts throughout the industrialized world. In fact, these problems appear to have extended the scope of policy-makers' interests in two significant directions. First, there has been increased interest in efforts to coordinate economic targets internationally. Multilaterally, this was the purpose of such meetings as the 1977 London summit conference of the leaders of the world's seven leading industrial nations. Subsequently, the efforts of the U.S. Administration to convince West Germany and Japan to stimulate their economies reflect the United States' view that these countries were not setting their policies in a way consistent with the consensus of the London summit.[17] Bilaterally, the U.S. Ambassador to Canada, Thomas Enders,

---

[17] The suggestion for coordinated stimulative policies in leading industrial nations as a means of generating higher growth rates was first proposed by the OECD Secretariat in 1976.

has been advocating more active communication on economic management between the two countries, even if only on an informal basis.[18] Second, frustration in dealing with economic problems by means of conventional cyclical stabilization tools has generated new interest in defining and solving so-called structural problems. Two major problems attracting attention are how to adjust to higher energy prices and how to operate the economy with a larger share of the labor force comprised of young and relatively inexperienced workers.

Trade

International trade is vitally important to both Canada and the United States. On a per capita basis Canada has long been one of the world's leading trading nations, and Canadians are acutely aware that their country's economic performance depends significantly on that of its major trading partners, of which the United States is by far the most important. Canadian exports and imports each represented about 20 percent of GNP in 1977. Foreign trade is a much smaller component of the U.S. economy, but it has been increasing rapidly during the 1970s, and this has had an important impact on the attitude of the United States toward world economic patterns. The ratio of exports to GNP rose from 4.1 percent in 1971 to 6.3 percent in 1977, and the ratio of imports, from 4.6 to 8.3 percent.[19] This trend has made the United States much more conscious that growth in the international economy is essential to the attainment of domestic economic objectives. At the various economic summits, in the OECD, the IMF, and the GATT, and in numerous other forums, the United States has joined with its major trading and financial partners in trying to devise compatible approaches to the difficult problems that now beset all economies. Whereas several years ago these initiatives could have been interpreted simply as the United States fulfilling its free-world-leadership obligations, they are now undertaken for reasons of direct economic self-interest.

Recently, the main source of concern in the area of world trade has been the dramatic increase in protectionist sentiment that has emerged in the countries of the Western industrialized world, particularly since the beginning of 1977. Officially, the governments of most of these countries are still committed to the principle of free trade. In practice, however, they have been responding to pressures from both the management and the labor groups involved in various threatened industries for protection against competition from foreign producers. The protection has been mostly in the form of non-tariff measures such as industrial subsidies, employment subsidies, voluntary

---

[18] See particularly Thomas O. Enders, "Canadians and Americans Are Facing the Same Economic Problems: We Can Do Something about Them Together," remarks to The Conference Board in Canada, Toronto, September 22, 1977.

[19] U.S. Department of Commerce, *International Economic Indicators*, *op. cit.*, p. 60.

export quotas, and discriminatory government procurement practices[20] While the term "protection" is usually used, those in threatened industries, particularly those in the labor movement, have claimed that all they are really seeking is "fair" trade conditions internationally. It is because they perceive an absence of such conditions that they say they require special assistance.

The large-scale emergence of protectionist sentiment can be traced partly to the persistent economic problems the developed countries have been facing. Aggregate demand has been slack for so long that some countries have begun selling goods in foreign markets at or below cost. This has created an immediate threat to the domestic businesses operating in these markets and to the jobs that these industries provide. This cyclical problem has been compounded by structural change. Developing countries — especially advanced developing countries such as Taiwan, South Korea, and Brazil — have been emerging as increasingly important sources of low-cost manufactured goods. This has caused further pressure on the supply-demand balance in a number of markets. It is worth noting that the capital for production facilities in these countries is often provided by investors in developed countries, attracted there by low labor costs. In principle, the developed countries have been working toward improving their markets for exports from developing countries. Leaders of the industrialized countries have indicated their willingness to expand their trade ties with developing countries in such recent international forums as the UNCTAD Conference in Nairobi in 1976 and the Conference on International Economic Cooperation (CIEC), which ran from December, 1975, to June, 1977.

Protectionist sentiment has been strong in a number of sectors in both Canada and the United States. During 1977 the U.S. government negotiated with foreign countries for cutbacks on imports of television sets and shoes; and on March 1, 1978, it implemented a complex system of "reference pricing" for steel imports designed to curtail dumping. The Canadian government imposed global quotas on footwear in December, 1977, and also took action in early 1978 to monitor steel imports so that possible dumping could be headed off.

Ironically, the growth of protectionist sentiment has been taking place against a background of official attempts to promote freer trade — the Tokyo Round of multilateral trade negotiations under way in Geneva. In fact, it is possible that the growth of protectionism has helped propel the MTN, which seemed to be getting bogged down; the protectionist threat has demonstrated very clearly how important the MTN is and has motivated those supporting it to

---

[20]Traditionally, tariffs have been the most widely used form of protection for domestic producers. Owing to the general lowering of tariff rates during the Kennedy Round of trade negotiations in the 1960s, however, policy-makers have been turning to non-tariff instruments.

get the proceedings moving.[21] The governments of Canada and the United States strongly support trade liberalization at the MTN — although, as will be shown in a fuller discussion in Chapter 3, their proposals have some significant differences.

A successful outcome to the current MTN must be considered very important. Not only is agreement needed to establish guidelines for world trade in the 1980s, but a failure of the negotiations would reflect badly on the ability of the Western industrialized countries to work together and would likely mean that *ad hoc* solutions would have to be worked out between individual countries, with some obviously not able to benefit as much as others. Combined with the existing protectionist sentiment, failure of the MTN could result in a serious breakdown in trading relations that would be most damaging to the world economy. The volume of international trade has grown tremendously in the past thirty years, and the world economy has benefited greatly from the international specialization that this trade has made possible.

Canadian Unity

Any review of Canada-U.S. relations made in 1978 would be incomplete without reference to the very serious internal-unity problem Canada faces as a result of the possibility that the province of Quebec will seek, in a forthcoming referendum, to obtain public support for its independence. This became the foremost political issue in Canada when the Parti Québécois (PQ), a political party dedicated to sovereignty for Quebec (with some sort of a continuing economic association with Canada), was elected to form the government of Quebec on November 15, 1976.

While the election of the PQ took many Canadians by surprise, the existence of widespread nationalist sentiment in Quebec was well-known. As a French-speaking region on an otherwise English-speaking continent, Quebec had remained for generations largely a rural society dominated by the clergy and other traditional elites. The industrial, commercial, and financial activity that took place in Montreal and other Quebec centers was primarily controlled by an English-speaking minority. During the 1960s, a period referred to now as the "Quiet Revolution," Quebec experienced a rapid social transition, marked particularly by a reorganization of the objectives of the educational system. French Canadians began to assert their desire to join the economic mainstream, and especially to have

---

[21] The launching of the current round of trade negotiations in Tokyo in September, 1973, was followed shortly by the OPEC oil-price increase. The series of world economic problems and reactions to them that resulted prompted many influential groups within the major negotiating countries to reappraise their trade-policy goals. Momentum for the MTN was lost and was restored only in 1977, notably because of the emphasis placed on trade in the declaration emanating from the London summit in May, which led to the timetable's being accelerated.

access to management and other higher-paying positions. At the same time, they felt they should be able to achieve these goals without foregoing their language and their culture, which they had maintained for over three hundred years. While virtually all French Canadians supported these goals in the interest of preserving Quebec's "national" identity, among the more radical there emerged the belief that they would be achieved only if Quebec were independent from Canada. It was from the union of three main independentist groups that the PQ was formed in 1968.[22]

In the election in which it gained power, the PQ, capitalizing on the difficulties of the previous government in managing the economy and dealing with labor problems, campaigned on behalf of good government rather than independence. It won 71 of the 110 seats in the National Assembly and received 40 percent of the popular vote.[23] The question of Quebec's independence is to be submitted to a referendum which the PQ has committed itself to holding sometime within its present term of office (which could run until 1981).

The record of the Parti Québécois government since taking office has been somewhat checkered. Relatively little has happened on the subject of the referendum, other than the introduction of a law dealing with the process by which it will be held. On the more fundamental question of what form the PQ wants Quebec's independence to take, there is considerable uncertainty. What is clear is that the PQ demands complete sovereignty from Canada, but wishes to negotiate various economic and other ties with the rest of Canada. Part of the reason that the terms of these ties have not been specified is that they are viewed by the PQ as the outcome of a bargaining process that it assumes the rest of Canada will engage in. The action that has undoubtedly attracted the most attention in the first year and a half has been the passage of the charter of the French language (commonly referred to as Bill 101), which greatly restricts access to education in English and makes French the only official language of the province, and hence discriminates against the use of

---

[22]The three were the essentially right-wing Ralliement National, the left-wing Rassemblement pour l'Indépendance Nationale, and the Mouvement Souveraineté Association, led by René Lévesque, a man who commanded sufficient political experience and respect to pull these groups together around a common interest. Tensions still exist in the Parti Québécois because of the fundamental differences in the philosophies of its members.

[23]In 1970 and 1973, the two previous provincial elections in which it had run candidates, the PQ had won widespread support, finishing second to the Liberal party both times in terms of popular vote. However, this popular support did not translate into many seats. In 1970 the PQ obtained 23 percent of the vote but only 7 seats, while the other major parties, the Union Nationale and the Créditistes, gained 17 and 12 seats, respectively, with only 20 and 10 percent of the popular vote. The Liberal party won the election with 72 seats and 46 percent of the vote. In 1973 the PQ increased its share of the popular vote to 30 percent but won only 6 seats. Still, this was sufficient to make it the Official Opposition, as the Liberal party won 102 of the total of 110 seats.

English in business operations.[24] The PQ government has also passed legislation amending the labor code, including measures making it much more difficult for a business to continue to operate when its employees are striking. At the same time, the first two budgets brought down by the PQ are generally conceded to have been appropriate for the economic conditions, imaginative, and fiscally quite responsible.[25] There is also an apparent determination to limit wage claims in the public sector by having settlements follow, rather than lead, average rates in the private sector. Whether the government will be able to achieve this goal is not yet clear, but its statement of objective, combined with the budgets, has somewhat eased the fears of many about its perceived socialist tendencies.

Reactions by the business community to the performance of the PQ have so far focused mainly on the language legislation. A number of businesses located in Quebec that operate nationally or internationally, for example, are finding that the restrictions on access to English schools are making it difficult to recruit necessary personnel from other parts of Canada and to get employees to transfer to Quebec. This is one reason why some firms, especially the head offices of large companies, have been moving part of their operations out of Quebec. In addition, one major company, the Sun Life Assurance Company of Canada, has announced it will be moving its head office entirely out of Quebec, citing as a reason that the language legislation would make operating there too difficult. (Sun Life made its decision before the regulations under Bill 101 pertaining to business operations were published.)

The problem of Quebec in Canada has occupied center stage and is related to a larger Canadian constitutional question. During the post-World War II period, the balance between the provincial and the federal governments has been under pressure throughout Canada. Both levels of government have been expanding, in response to changes in societal demands, in such areas as regulation of communications and consumer protection. This has led to duplication of services and, in some cases, to conflicts between levels of government. In addition, the federal government has made funds available to the provinces that have made it attractive for them to initiate programs they otherwise might not have become involved in to

---

[24] With some exceptions, the charter restricts schooling in English to students whose parents were educated in the English school system in Quebec or who already have a brother or sister attending school in English. The law also provides for sanctions to be imposed on medium- and large-scale businesses in Quebec if they do not obtain a certificate that they are conducting their operations in French.

[25] The main exception to this assessment of the PQ's budgets, a concern that has been expressed by a number of executives of Quebec-based companies, is that they have been raising the income tax burden on people in the upper income range relative to that in other parts of Canada, and this can be expected to make it more difficult for businesses in Quebec to keep top professional and management people and to attract new ones.

the same extent.[26] Canada is a strongly regionalized country, and the effect of federal government decisions on the operations of the provincial governments has upset areas of the country other than Quebec. There continues to be widespread suspicion in both the western and the eastern provinces, for instance, that to a considerable extent the economic disparities that exist in Canada and the uneven distribution of the industrial base have been shaped by biases in federal government policies going back many years. Given this broader context to the question of Canadian unity, it is difficult to know how much of the dissatisfaction of Quebecers with their situation is linguistic and cultural and how much is economic.

What Canada presently faces is an urgent need to reassess the division of powers among the various levels of government. The Canadian Constitution was originally based on the notion that the division of such powers should accommodate the individual needs of the various regions of the country. It has become increasingly evident that the present system is incapable of achieving this goal and that a somewhat different division of powers is needed. This may or may not require a new constitutional framework.[27] If constitutional changes are necessary, however, they will undoubtedly take a number of years to achieve because the necessary formula for amending Canada's Constitution is far from clear.[28] The existence of such serious dissatisfaction with the current division of powers in Canada as a whole suggests that defeat of the Quebec referendum would need to be accompanied by real changes in powers if the aspirations of Quebec and the other regions are to be met.

Although Americans have been following the situation in Quebec with great interest, U.S. government officials have been careful to point out that the United States considers this to be an internal Canadian matter and one in which it does not intend to interfere. Nevertheless, two areas in particular are of concern to Americans. One has to do with the economic implications. Americans

---

[26]The federal government took a major step toward easing difficulties in this area when it passed into law on April 1, 1977, the Federal-Provincial Fiscal Arrangements and Established Programmes Financing Act, which separates its funding of programs from the contributions of the provinces and substitutes instead block grants to the provinces.

[27]On June 12, 1978, the federal government issued a policy paper on constitutional reform as a first step in a process it hopes will sort out the question of the division of powers (Government of Canada, *A Time for Action: Toward the Renewal of the Canadian Federation* [Ottawa: Supply and Services Canada, 1978]).

[28]Efforts by Canada's political leaders during the past decade to find a formula for amending Canada's Constitution have revealed that it will be extremely difficult to arrive at a procedure that will safeguard provincial and individual rights while providing sufficient flexibility to meet the changing economic, social, and political needs of the future. Another obstacle is that Canada may also have to deal with "repatriating" its Constitution, since what is commonly referred to as Canada's Constitution, the British-North America Act of 1867, is an act of the Parliament of the United Kingdom.

have extensive investments, both in equity and in debt forms, in all parts of Canada, and they are naturally following closely the effects of developments in Quebec on the investment climate throughout the country, with their implications for existing and possible future investment. U.S. businessmen have already expressed apprehension over the leftist position of the Quebec government as indicated by its decision to take over a major operator in the asbestos industry and by its policy to disallow foreign investment in certain vital sectors.[29] In addition, because Canada is its largest trading partner, the United States is concerned about the effect that the situation in Quebec may be having on Canada's overall economic health. The second principal area of U.S. concern is the possible implications for the North American defense system of a separate Quebec. In its early years the Parti Québécois tended to endorse a posture of non-alignment with the major power blocs, but more recently it has indicated a pro-Western-alliance attitude.

The Bilateral Focus

While this chapter has concentrated on the major problems faced by Canada and the United States in the past two years and on the policy responses of each country, the analysis does suggest some conclusions relevant to the current tone of bilateral relations. Because of the international scope of the problems of energy, economic performance, and trade, there has been a tendency for the two countries to look to one another for support in finding solutions. The sense of common concern that has emerged has made the two countries more willing to cooperate with one another, not only in dealing with these common problems, but also, as the next three chapters will show, in dealing with areas of bilateral conflict. Consistent with this overall shift in emphasis toward these fundamental problem areas, each country has felt less at liberty to pursue the individual policy initiatives that in the past had caused bilateral irritation. In addition, bilateral frictions have largely been pushed off the front pages by strictly domestic matters — in Canada, for example, by the question of national unity. The environment created by these international and domestic concerns has ultimately made it somewhat easier for officials of the two countries to sort out bilateral difficulties.

---

[29] Quebec government officials have argued that Quebec's policy toward foreign investment would be less restrictive overall than that created by the Canadian government's Foreign Investment Review Agency.

3

Bilateral Trade Issues*

Trade is one of the most important expressions of the economic relationship between Canada and the United States. Each country is the other's major partner for both exports and imports, with bilateral trade accounting for about 70 percent of Canadian, and about 20 percent of U.S., exports and imports. The value of this trade — about $60 billion in 1977 — makes this bilateral trading relationship the world's largest.

This chapter will look at specific issues that have arisen in the past two years as a result of this trading relationship, but first it is worthwhile to review the major trends in the trade balance between the two countries. As indicated in Chapter 2, the overall current-account balances of both Canada and the United States were in deficit in 1976 and 1977. In terms of the merchandise trade between the two countries, Canada had a surplus in 1976 and 1977 — and indeed in every year since 1970, with the exception of 1975. Official Canadian and U.S. data on the size of the Canadian surplus vary considerably, however. Table 2 shows the extent of the discrepancy and also provides the results of a joint exercise by the two governments to reconcile the merchandise-trade data. This series, starting with 1970 statistics, has recently been discontinued, at least temporarily. The United States does not regard its deficit with Canada as a major contributor to its recent overall deficit — trade with Japan and increasing oil imports are considered more important proximate causes — but Canada stands to be affected by any generalized remedial measures.

With respect to non-merchandise, or services, trade, Canada had a large deficit with the United States in 1976 and 1977 — a deficit that, as Table 3 shows, has existed since 1970. Canada's net payments to the United States for the major non-merchandise element, interest and dividends, increased appreciably in 1976 and 1977. At the same time, however, the U.S. share of the overall Canadian deficit on interest and dividends declined to 80 percent in 1977 from

---

*This chapter was prepared by Sperry Lea of the staff of the National Planning Association.

TABLE 2

Canadian-U.S. Merchandise Trade, 1970-77[a]

	1970	1971	1972	1973	1974	1975	1976	1977
U.S. trade with Canada (bil. U.S. $):								
U.S. exports	9.1	10.4	12.4	15.1	19.9	21.7	24.1	25.7
U.S. imports	11.1	12.7	14.9	17.7	21.9	21.7	26.2	29.3
U.S. balance	−2.0	−2.3	−2.5	−2.6	−2.0	0.0	−2.1	−3.6
Canadian trade with U.S. (bil. Can. $):								
Canadian exports	11.0	12.2	14.1	17.3	21.7	21.9	25.6	31.0
Canadian imports	9.8	10.7	12.6	16.1	20.7	23.1	25.2	29.3
Canadian balance	1.1	1.4	1.5	1.2	1.0	−1.1	0.4	1.7
Reconciled figures (bil. U.S. $):								
U.S. exports	9.1	10.6	12.6	16.1	21.1	22.8	25.5	n.a.
U.S. imports	10.6	12.0	14.2	17.3	22.1	21.4	26.2	n.a.
U.S. balance	−1.4	−1.5	−1.5	−1.2	−0.9	1.3	−0.7	

[a]Totals do not always add because of rounding.

Sources: United States: U.S. Department of Commerce, *U.S. Trade with Major Trading Partners, 1970-76* (Washington, D.C., September, 1977), pp. 11, 13, and 15, plus 1977 estimates furnished by the Department.
Canada: Statistics Canada, *Quarterly Estimates of the Canadian Balance of International Payments*, Fourth Quarter, 1977 (Ottawa, 1978), p. 63.

96 percent in 1975, owing to more than a tenfold increase in Canada's annual net payments to other countries.[1] The second major problem area for Canada has been its travel account, which has shifted from a positive balance with the United States during the first half of the decade into a deficit position over the past three years. While this can be explained partly by abnormal occurrences (for example, the $610 million deficit in 1976 can be attributed largely to the U.S. bicentennial year plus a strike affecting air travel in Canada), some longer-range trends are also at work, particularly the increasing habit of Canadians to take winter vacations in the southern United States. Another factor, discussed later in this chapter, is the recent U.S. convention tax, which is claimed to have cost Canada $100-200 million in 1977.

Two other points deserve mention. First, manufactured products comprise about 80 percent of U.S. exports to Canada and over 40 percent of Canadian exports to the United States.[2] Underlying the

---

[1] This reflects the diversion of major Canadian borrowing away from the United States during the past two years, an occurrence described in Chapter 4.

[2] That manufactured goods were 41.6 percent of total Canadian exports to the United States (as compiled by Statistics Canada, *Summary of External Trade*, December, 1977 [Ottawa, 1978], p. 37) represents an important accomplishment. Before 1960, manufactured goods exports were about 10 percent; between 1960 and 1965 they doubled, and by 1969 they had doubled again. The Automotive Agreement was the single most important reason, but if auto trade is disregarded, other manufactures still doubled their shares during the 1960s.

TABLE 3

Balance of Canada's Non-Merchandise Trade and Its Major Elements, 1970-77
(million Canadian dollars)

	1970	1971	1972	1973	1974	1975	1976	1977
All non-merchandise trade:								
Total balance	−2,099	−2,398	−2,527	−2,971	−3,765	−4,635	−5,798	−7,517
With United States	−1,348	−1,660	−1,785	−2,172	−2,677	−3,740	−4,599	−5,646
With others	−751	−738	−742	−799	−1,088	−895	−1,199	−1,871
Interest and dividends:								
Total balance	−1,022	−1,141	−1,048	−1,260	−1,555	−1,918	−2,491	−3,413
With United States	−970	−1,081	−1,038	−1,233	−1,481	−1,849	−2,083	−2,716
With others	−52	−60	−10	−27	−74	−69	−408	−697
Travel account:								
Total balance	−216	−202	−234	−296	−284	−727	−1,191	−1,655
With United States	156	194	104	87	132	−250	−610	−769
With others	−372	−396	−338	−383	−416	−477	−581	−886

Source: Statistics Canada, *Quarterly Estimates of the Canadian Balance of International Payments, op. cit.*, pp. 62-63.

two-way trade in manufactures is the important fact that a large portion of it now consists of similar, or even identical, items produced on both sides of the border by U.S. companies. These companies often have the option of producing a given product in either country; this is especially true for the U.S. automotive industry, where location decisions have again become a highly controversial issue.

Second, evaluating bilateral trade solely by its dollar balance carries the false implication that the only issue is the balance itself. But to Canadians and Americans, and thus to those representing them in Parliament and Congress, the job implications of bilateral trade are more directly meaningful, especially during a time of concern over high unemployment. This, plus the above-mentioned similarity of many of the manufactured items being traded across the border, explains why bilateral trade issues are considered in balance-of-jobs terms, as well as in dollar balances, notwithstanding the great difficulties in authenticating such effects statistically.

This chapter groups trends and issues with bilateral significance that have emerged over the past two years into four sections: automotive trade, the permanently dominating feature in bilateral trade and its traditionally most reliable incubator of issues; the current multilateral trade negotiations, the results of which will have a significant impact on future bilateral trade; two unconnected events affecting service transactions — the Canadian measures on cross-border TV advertising and the U.S. convention tax — which arose as separate major issues during the past two years, and for which the attempt to link solutions may make for a still larger issue; and, finally, Canada's process for acquiring a new fighter aircraft. Recent bilateral trade developments involving energy and other resource materials are covered in Chapter 5.

Automotive Trade

Any way you look at it, the automotive industry is the dominant sector in Canadian-U.S. economic interaction. Auto production employs directly well over one million persons in the two countries, and several times that number indirectly. It provides the major markets for basic materials such as lead, synthetic rubber, iron, steel, and aluminum and is virtually the only market for innumerable supplier industries.

The importance of the auto sector in Canada-U.S. trade stems from the Canada-U.S. Automotive Agreement of 1965, as a result of which new vehicles and parts for incorporation into them have risen from a small item in bilateral trade to by far the largest, accounting for roughly one-third of each country's exports to the other. (Auto imports from Europe and Japan account for roughly 20 percent of the North American market.)

An apparently indelible birthmark of the Automotive Agreement has been disagreement over what is meant by its announced goal of "enabling the industries of both countries to participate on a fair and equitable basis in the expanding total market of the two countries."[3] Each side continually scrutinizes its bilateral trade balance carefully and watches the division of the benefits from production activity in terms of employment, investment, and, particularly in Canada's case, research and development expenditures. Whenever this analysis reveals a sharp turn against one country or a persistent adverse result, calls are made to renegotiate the Agreement. In the early years, when the trade balance swung in Canada's favor, such calls were heard in the U.S. Congress; more recently, most of the complaints have come from Canada as the trade surplus has shifted to the United States; concerns have also mounted about the quality of the automotive activity taking place in Canada — for example, in terms of the skill levels of jobs available to Canadians.

Two concerns over the distribution of automotive production between Canada and the United States have attracted considerable attention in the past two years; one involves the recorded trade balance in auto parts and the other is the question of where large-scale new investment in the auto industry will be located.

The Auto-Parts-Balance Question

The joint official record of automotive trade between Canada and the United States shows a widening deficit for Canada in automotive parts trade (see Table 4). While Canada has had a sufficient surplus in the trade in assembled vehicles that the overall balance in 1976 and 1977 was actually better than in 1974 and 1975, the large and continuously expanding deficit in parts has recently contributed to a widespread sentiment in Canada that the goals of the Automotive Agreement are not being met.

In early 1977 the Automotive Parts Manufacturers' Association of Canada proposed changes to the Agreement that would set a limit on Canada's parts deficit and promote new production and employment in Canada. By the fall of that year, the federal government had indicated it was working on a strategy to redress Canada's position under the auto pact.[4] One possibility was to establish a special

---

[3] *Agreement Concerning Automotive Products Between the Government of the United States of America and the Government of Canada*, Appendix A. The equitable-participation question and its frequent incompatibility with another proclaimed objective of the Agreement — greater production efficiency in both countries — are discussed at length in Chapter 4 of Canadian-American Committee, *A Time of Difficult Transitions: Canada-U.S. Relations in 1976* (Montreal and Washington, 1976), pp. 25-39.

[4] Speech by Gordon Osbaldeston, Deputy Minister of the Canadian Department of Industry, Trade and Commerce, to a conference of the Automotive Parts Manufacturers' Association of Canada, Toronto, October 27, 1977.

TABLE 4

U.S. Automotive Trade Balance with Canada, 1970-77
(million U.S. dollars)

	1970	1971	1972	1973	1974	1975	1976	1977
Cars and trucks	−1,144	−1,192	−1,199	−979	−909	−662	−1,501	−1,924
Parts	939	967	1,071	1,380	1,983	2,401	2,567	2,938
Tires and tubes	9	28	29	24	158	103	−50	9
Automotive balance	−196	−197	−99	426	1,233	1,892	1,016	1,023

Sources: Through 1976, derived from data in *Eleventh Annual Report . . . of the Operation of the Automotive Products Trade Act of 1965* (Washington, D.C.: Senate Finance Committee, 1977). Preliminary 1977 data added by U.S. Department of Commerce.

auto investment corporation to make or guarantee loans to Canadian auto parts producers.[5] The government of the Province of Ontario also got into the act with the release of a study that concluded that Canadian parts activity was "significantly below a 'fair share.' "[6] (The majority of Canadian vehicle assembly and parts manufacturing takes place in Ontario.)

The only concrete move the Canadian government has made, however, favors domestic parts production for use in vehicles not covered by the Automotive Agreement. A plan has been implemented by which a foreign automobile manufacturer can apply for remission of a portion of the 15 percent duty on vehicles exported to Canada equal to the value of the parts purchased in Canada by the manufacturer. One company requesting this duty-remission scheme was Volkswagen of Canada Ltd., a subsidiary of Volkswagenwerk AG of West Germany, which in early 1978 opened its first North American assembly plant in Pennsylvania. Previously, Canadian duty remissions were allowed only up to the value of parts in vehicles actually exported to Canada, so it is envisaged that the change will stimulate Canadian parts production. The U.S. government has indicated that it opposes the duty-remission plan, and officials of the two countries have met to discuss the issue.[7] It was a similar duty-remission

---

[5] This possibility was revealed by Jack Horner, the Minister of Industry, Trade and Commerce (see *Globe and Mail* [Toronto], April 21, 1978). A further indication of the Canadian government's concern over the automotive industry was revealed in June, 1978, when the government announced the launching of a major inquiry into the industry under the direction of Simon Reisman, a former Deputy Minister of Finance and closely involved in the original negotiation of the Automotive Agreement.

[6] Ontario Ministry of Treasury, Economics and Intergovernmental Affairs, *Canada's Share of the North American Automotive Industry: An Ontario Perspective* (Toronto, 1978), p. i.

[7] See the statement by C. Fred Bergsten, Assistant Secretary of the Treasury for International Affairs, before the International Trade, Investment and Monetary Policy

scheme by Canada in 1962 that provided much of the motivation for the 1965 Automotive Agreement.

Canada's concern over its bilateral auto parts deficit has also provoked a closer look at the data. Several conceptual anomalies have been identified, the elimination of which would change the balance in one direction or the other, in some cases drastically.

• Parts trade data include not only original equipment parts, which are covered by the Automotive Agreement, but also parts for the replacement market, which are not. The effect on Canada's parts deficit of counting only parts for new vehicles would be to reduce it slightly.[8]

• A significant share of original equipment parts received by either country from the other are not truly imported, since they soon return incorporated in new vehicles. Eliminating the estimated value of all such repatriated parts, both from each country's parts imports and from its vehicle exports, would not change the overall automotive trade balance. However, the adjustment would reduce Canada's present parts deficit by enough (over $3 billion) to create a modest surplus, meanwhile subtracting this amount from its vehicle surplus to produce a deficit.[9]

• A similar but far smaller adjustment would remove the estimated value of those imported parts that are re-exported to third countries within new vehicles. The elimination of re-exported parts on both sides would reduce Canada's auto parts deficit while not affecting the vehicle balance.[10]

• The two previous adjustments involve only those parts traded as such. Adding the value of parts that are made in either country

---

Subcommittee of the House Committee on Banking, Finance and Urban Affairs on August 1, 1978 (Department of the Treasury, *News*, August 1, 1978).

[8] Canada's deficits on original equipment parts only in 1976 and 1977 were U.S.$2,404 million and U.S.$2,812 million, thus U.S.$163 million and U.S.$125 million lower than the figures for these years in Table 4 (data obtained from U.S. Department of Commerce).

[9] This kind of adjustment was first suggested by officials of the Ford Motor Company of Canada in December, 1976. It is discussed in Standing Senate Committee on Foreign Affairs, *Canada's Trade Relations with the United States* (Ottawa: Queen's Printer, 1978), pp. 99 and 149. Computations by Committee staff show that eliminating repatriated parts would have improved Canada's parts balance in 1976 and 1977 by U.S.$3.3 billion and U.S.$3.8 billion while subtracting these values from its vehicle surplus. These large amounts stem from the fact that Canada imports twice the value of parts from the United States and exports ten times as great a share of its vehicle production than vice versa; thus the value of parts repatriated via Canada is twenty times that repatriated via the United States.

[10] For further comment on this adjustment, see Ontario Ministry of Treasury, Economics and Intergovernmental Affairs, *op. cit.*, pp. 7-11. The value of the adjustment can be only roughly estimated, owing to the fact that overseas exports include assembled and unassembled vehicles; but given the volumes and shares of vehicle production involved, Canada's parts balance would now be improved by $300-500 million (author's estimate).

and incorporated there into vehicles exported to the other country would considerably enlarge Canada's parts deficit with the United States. It would, however, improve Canada's vehicle surplus by the same amount.[11]

• At least one major anomaly exists in the detailed U.S. statistics for auto parts imported from Canada. Of over one hundred separate categories, by far the largest — accounting for over 40 percent in total value in 1976 and 1977 — includes truck tractors that have large trailer rigs. The planned reclassification of truck tractors as vehicles would enlarge Canada's parts deficit and improve its vehicle surplus.

In terms of total automotive trade, it is clear that Canada has a deficit with the United States. Until there is an agreement on which, if any, adjustments should be made in the parts trade data, it is not clear what role the parts balance plays in the total picture. It is debatable, moreover, whether it is in keeping with the spirit of the Automotive Agreement to break out the balances for particular subsections in this way. A better basis for gauging the distribution of parts production between the two countries — the root of Canada's present concern — would be the value added in plants principally engaged in this activity. Such a measure of actual in-plant production would, when compared with the consumption of auto parts in each country, provide a relatively straightforward base for any judgment of how fairly parts production is being allocated between them. The problem with this approach is that value added may be even more complex to calculate than trade statistics.

Investment in the Automotive Industry

U.S. government requirements for more fuel-efficient cars have recently set into motion developments that will change the North American automotive industry significantly. The Energy Policy and Conservation Act of 1975 stipulates that, for the U.S. market, the sales-weighted average gas mileage for cars offered by each firm must reach 18 miles per gallon by 1978 and 27.5 miles per gallon by 1985. The design problems this raises are compounded by other U.S. regulations for safety and engine emissions, whose solutions often work against better fuel economy. For the next few years the only design path that can meet the mileage targets is weight reduction, achievable mainly by making cars smaller, although substituting lighter materials can help. Radical energy-saving changes in engines cannot be expected until the 1980s. Regardless of public preference, therefore, producers will increasingly offer the smaller, typically

---

[11]The Standing Senate Committee on Foreign Affairs (op. cit., p. 150) concludes that this adjustment would have increased Canada's auto parts deficit for 1975 by about $2 billion. It suggests combining this and the second adjustment noted above, which together would leave Canada with a reduced parts deficit.

front-wheel-drive "world cars" such as the Volkswagen "Rabbit," contemporary Japanese cars, the Ford "Fiesta," the GM "Chevette," and Chrysler Corporation's "Horizon"/"Omni" (to use their North American names).

The design changeover will result in a more competitive situation for manufacturers serving the U.S. market, posing a particular challenge for U.S. and Canadian operations of the four U.S. auto firms because it will eliminate what has been in effect a formidable and perfectly legal barrier against widespread foreign imports: the fact that the U.S. firms alone mass-produce what the North American market has traditionally preferred — the full-size, moderately priced "North American family car." The challenge now facing these North American plants is thus not from import penetration in the traditional form of small foreign cars winning markets from their larger cars. Rather, it will be head-to-head competition in world cars being mass-produced by ten or so major international firms domiciled in the United States, Europe, and Japan that can distribute their operations widely among industrialized countries and increasingly in certain low-wage developing countries.

The question is thus whether North American production can maintain a major share of its home market for what will now be a standard manufactured product, a challenge it has found difficult to meet with items such as color TV sets. Several definite signs point to large-scale auto production's remaining in North America. Partially stimulated by the decline in the dollar, Volkswagen has already begun mass production in Pennsylvania, while several Japanese firms are reported to be looking into the prospects for auto production in various North American locations. Starting in 1980, U.S. fuel-efficiency regulations will discourage U.S. manufacturers from producing, other than in North America, small cars for the U.S. market.[12] Most significantly, U.S. firms are said to be planning to invest $60-70 billion over the next seven or eight years for new plants and retooling.[13]

Any decision about where large new investment expenditures in North America will be made comes face to face with the old question of what "fair and equitable" market shares should mean under the terms of the Canada-U.S. Automotive Agreement. Both governments have shown themselves sensitive to this issue. Jack Horner, the Canadian Minister of Industry, Trade and Commerce, has noted that Canada accounts for close to 10 percent of North American vehicle sales and has suggested that new investment in Canada should

---

[12] After 1980 at least 75 percent of the value of a car must have been added in the United States or Canada for it to count toward a company's mileage average.

[13] According to *The Economist* (June 10, 1978, pp. 91-92), investment will be $58 billion over the next eight years, of which General Motors will account for $30 billion and Ford, $20 billion. *Business Week* (June 19, 1978, pp. 26-27) suggests $70 billion will be invested over the next seven years.

reflect the relative importance of the Canadian market.[14] However, there is concern that the North American automobile manufacturers will concentrate new investment in the United States.[15] The U.S. government, meanwhile, has been concerned by the incentives that the various levels of government in Canada have offered the automobile companies to get them to locate new facilities in Canada. In early August, 1978, it was revealed that, with $40 million in assistance promised by the federal government, and $28 million by the Government of Ontario, Ford had decided to locate a new engine plant in Ontario. In addition, the federal government indicated in May, 1978, that it would be willing, through grants covered by the Department of Regional Economic Expansion, to commit $60 million of federal money to go along with $20 million from the Quebec government in an effort to persuade General Motors to locate an aluminum die-casting plant in Quebec. While recognizing that some states have also been wooing domestic and foreign automobile manufacturers, the U.S. government has expressed disapproval that in Canada "these interventionist practices are escalating to the federal level."[16] Canadian and U.S. government officials met to discuss the incentives issue on August 4, 1978, and it is reported that both sides agreed efforts should be made to avoid a bidding war to attract automotive manufacturing.[17]

The Multilateral Trade Negotiations

Not all the developments important to bilateral trade involve only the two countries. Indeed, the successful outcome of the "Tokyo Round" of multilateral trade negotiations (MTN) could have a major impact on the volume and composition of Canada-U.S. trade and could help resolve several long-standing bilateral non-tariff problems.

During the past two years no more crucial question for the future conduct of Canada-U.S. trade arose than whether the will to

[14] Department of Industry, Trade and Commerce, News Release, June 16, 1978.

[15] Canadian fears about the direction of the Canadian auto-assembly and parts-manufacturing industries were contained in a Canadian government study that paralleled one by the U.S. government, the two having been initiated jointly by Prime Minister Trudeau and President Ford in December, 1974. The Canadian report (Automotive Task Force, *Review of the North American Automotive Industry* [Ottawa: Department of Industry, Trade and Commerce, 1977]) devoted considerable attention to the structure of the industry in North America, with major emphasis on the auto parts sector. The U.S. study (U.S. Department of Commerce, *Impact of Environmental, Energy and Safety Regulations and of Emerging Market Factors upon the U.S. Sector of the North American Automotive Industry* [Washington, D.C.: U.S. Government Printing Office, 1977]) concentrated on how and by when manufacturers for the U.S. car market can alter their models to satisfy the new regulations.

[16] Bergsten, *op. cit.*

[17] *Globe and Mail* (Toronto), August 5, 1978.

proceed with the MTN would be overpowered by the protectionist drift among industrialized countries. Two developments in 1977 signaled rededication by the major participants: the "Downing Street Declaration" emanating from the London economic summit meeting in May, which asserted the wish of political leaders to see progress achieved quickly, and the positive response to the subsequent U.S. call to accelerate the timetable and to force decisions on a number of sticky points. This schedule successfully met its first test when participating countries presented their specific tariff "offers" in January, 1978. A second major step was taken when a "framework of understanding" for concluding the MTN, supported by twenty leading industrialized countries, was reached at a ministerial meeting in July, 1978. The communiqué from the subsequent Bonn summit charged negotiators to "resolve the outstanding issues and to conclude successfully the detailed negotiations by December 15, 1978."

It will be possible to assess the bilateral implications of the MTN only after the smoke has cleared from the negotiations. However, over the past two years certain broad features of the two countries' positions have become evident.

Canada has set for itself the specific objective of gaining better access to foreign markets for semi-processed and manufactured products derived from its natural resources — in particular, forest products, non-ferrous metal products, and petrochemicals. While its major market for these products will remain the United States, Canada sees considerable potential in Europe if the relevant tariffs and non-tariff measures there can be significantly lowered. In this quest, however, Canada's proposal to negotiate by sectors, which would have served its objectives, was rejected and replaced by a tariff-cutting formula that does not. With the essential bargaining in the MTN being among the United States, the European Economic Community, and Japan, Canada has recognized that it holds comparatively low cards and that it "will have to play its hand with great skill to come out ahead."[18]

The U.S. objectives for the MTN are concentrated mainly on the effects of the MTN on U.S. trade with the European Community and Japan and on more active trade-liberalizing measures by advanced developing countries such as Brazil. In all cases the question has been not merely how much better access to U.S. products these countries will offer, but how much more fairly they will conduct their own export trade. The United States appears less anxious than Canada about achieving its goals in the MTN, in part because it has far more bargaining power.

---

[18] Comment by reporter James Rusk in *Globe and Mail* (Toronto), March 29, 1978.

Tariff Cutting

Meaningful negotiations to reduce import duties were held up until a general approach was adopted by participants in late 1977. This approach, the so-called Swiss Formula, seeks to harmonize tariffs through greater proportional reductions in the higher than in the lower rates. The participants have agreed to exchange with each other over an eight-year period a package of tariff cuts averaging 40 percent, but with the possibility of exempting certain items and making greater cuts in others than the formula requires. Since late 1977, negotiations on this basis have consisted of each participant's responding to specific trading requests from its partners by offering concessions that would be extended to all of them.

The Swiss Formula ill suits Canada's particular tariff structure and major objectives. It requires deeper cuts by Canada than by the other parties to the negotiations because Canada imposes a higher average level of tariffs on dutiable industrial imports.[19] At the same time, the formula requires from other countries minimal cuts in the comparatively low tariffs on the semi-processed items that form a large proportion of Canada's exports. Even though the actual tariff rates would be low, however, their "effective rates" would still be high enough to inhibit achievement of the Canadian goal of further processing of raw materials in Canada.[20] Thus Canada has sought, from the United States, the EEC, and Japan, "greater-than-formula" cuts in their low tariffs affecting a range of products where Canada considers itself competitive. The U.S. tariff-cutting offer made in June, 1978, met most of Canada's requests. It included elimination of U.S. duties under 5 percent on 120 products and the cutting of tariffs by up to 60 percent on other products with duties over 5 percent. The European and Japanese offers, however, have not come nearly as close to meeting Canada's requests.

U.S. interests in Canadian tariff concessions are less clearly defined by product area, except for machinery and petrochemicals. They tend to be oriented instead toward rather more technical long-term objectives — for example, that Canada "bind" more of its tariff rates on products of interest to the United States,[21] that it reduce

---

[19] Fifty-five percent of Canada's dutiable industrial imports from the United States, the EEC, and Japan are subject to duties over 10 percent, while 90 percent of Canada's dutiable exports to these countries are subject to duties at rates 10 percent or below (see Canadian Trade and Tariffs Committee, "Review of Developments in the GATT Multilateral Trade Negotiations in Geneva," mimeographed [August, 1977], p. 22).

[20] For example, suppose a raw material import faces no tariff, while after some slight processing a 4 percent tariff is applied. If that stage of processing adds 20 percent to the value of the raw material, it would raise its price from, say, $100 to $120. The tariff on the processed good is only $4.80 (that is, 4 percent of $120); but compared to the zero tariff on raw material, it is actually an effective tariff of 24 percent on the $20 worth of processing activity.

[21] "Binding" a tariff involves a commitment by the importing country to its principal

the disparities on specific items between its duties and the usually lower U.S. rates, and that it eliminate the practice whereby certain imports bear a second, higher duty if "of a class or kind" made in Canada.

The outcome for Canada-U.S. trade of tariff cutting in the MTN is in doubt at the time of writing. The final offers to be made by the two countries will depend on their reaching an agreed balance of concessions, not only with each other and on tariffs — which might not be difficult — but also with all their major trading partners and on changes in non-tariff measures.

Non-Tariff Distortions

During the past two years pre-negotiations were carried on with respect to government procurement, products standards, customs valuations, safeguards, and the especially important and difficult question of subsidies affecting exports coupled with the right of importing countries to reply with countervailing duties. The objective is to negotiate international codes of conduct for these various categories of non-tariff measures. In the Canada-U.S. context, specific requests and offers have been exchanged, but these are largely lost from view in the calculated obscurities of the negotiating process at work in an area of particular complexity and uncertain success.

For all that, the MTN activity with the greatest potential importance for Canada-U.S. trade could well be in the non-tariff area, because any further agreement toward international rules could head off misunderstandings that continue to occur. Three forms of non-tariff distortion appear particularly important to bilateral trade.

• The most sensitive bilateral area is *subsidies and countervailing duties.* An important aspect of a country's industrial policy may be the encouragement of industrial production in less favored regions, a process usually involving assistance in a variety of forms from various levels of government. When the output of a subsidized business is exported to another country, however, the assistance, although intended mainly to increase employment or to minimize regional disparities, may well be interpreted as constituting a subsidy that stimulates exports and be answered as such by a countervailing duty. The United States applies countervailing duties on dutiable imports without observing the GATT requirement to first find injury.

The classic example of this process in the bilateral context occurred in 1973, when the United States countervailed against Michelin tires imported from new production facilities in Nova Scotia — facilities that had benefited from assistance by the federal,

<hr />

supplier of a product not to raise the agreed tariff rate without first consulting that country and then strictly according to GATT rules.

provincial, and local governments and that would be exporting three-quarters of their production to the United States. More recently, the U.S. Treasury found in June, 1978, that a production subsidy to assist Canada's depressed east coast groundfish industry justified countervailing under U.S. law. Because of modifications agreed to by the Canadian government, however, Treasury has waived the right to do so under an authority that expires in January, 1979. Finally, on the basis of the investment incentives discussed above that are being offered to the major automobile manufacturing companies, the subsidy/countervail question seems to have become a major issue in the North American automotive industry.

For these reasons, Canadian-U.S. trade relations would be particularly favored by any progress in the MTN toward international agreement on defining a subsidy and toward distinguishing cases where these subsidies promote exports sufficient to justify a countervail and, in Canada's case, by the United States' agreeing to comply with the GATT requirements for finding injury on dutiable items before a countervailing duty can be applied. An indication of progress in these areas is two commitments in the "framework of understanding" that emerged from the July, 1978, GATT ministerial meeting: the recognition that "domestic as well as export subsidies can impair GATT benefits and bestow rights to take countermeasures" and the extension of this recognition "to both agricultural and industrial export subsidies."[22] If these commitments are carried out, they could ease bilateral difficulties in this area.

• The second non-tariff area of considerable relevance to Canadian-U.S. trade is *safeguards*. Article XIX of the GATT provides temporary import restrictions for an industry confronted by imports "in such increased quantities and under such conditions as to cause or threaten serious injury to domestic producers ... of like or directly competing products." Both Canada and the United States have used this provision in cases that turned out mainly to affect each other, even though bilateral trade was not the cause of the difficulties. In 1976 the Canadian government imposed import quotas on doubleknit fabric and on a wide variety of clothing — quotas that affected nearly 25 percent of all U.S. textile exports. In December, 1977, Canada followed somewhat the same action for footwear. In the same month U.S. zinc producers petitioned the International Trade Commission for an escape clause action against imports of zinc slab, a product of which Canada is the largest foreign supplier to the United States, but this was later rejected by the ITC.

One issue being negotiated in the MTN — whether safeguards can be applied selectively rather than against all exporters of the

---

[22] See testimony of Robert S. Strauss, Special Representative for Trade Negotiations, before the House Ways and Means Committee Subcommittee on Trade, July 18, 1978.

product in question — poses something of a dilemma for Canada and the United States. On the one hand, each of these countries has frequently hurt the other inadvertently when adopting safeguards against some other low-cost producer — textiles being a case in point — which argues for selective safeguards. On the other hand, this policy would violate the strong tradition in both countries to uphold the most-favored-nation doctrine of non-discrimination.

Another issue related to safeguards has proved to be an irritant to bilateral trade relations during the past two years. The United States maintains that the country applying temporary restrictions must offer temporary compensation to restore the "balance of concessions." Canada understands no such obligation to exist so long as the original action taken satisfies Article XIX. In the textile case, agreement regarding compensation was finally reached in September, 1977; Canada temporarily reduced or suspended import duties on about $127 million of imported U.S. fabrics, yarns, and fibers. Meanwhile, the footwear case now involves considerable disagreement as to whether Canada owes compensation. Again, progress in the MTN toward internationally acceptable rules would ease what proved to be a cause of friction over the past two years.

● The third area of non-tariff distortions is *government procurement*. Recent examples include procurement preferences in Quebec, British Columbia, Minnesota, Pennsylvania, Indiana, West Virginia, and Maryland, as well as certain U.S. federal legislation such as the Public Works Employment Act (1977) and the Clean Water Act (1977).[23] While the MTN might be helpful in discouraging such actions in North America, the problems are basically those of the relations of state and provincial actions to federal law in the two countries on matters affecting trade.

TV Advertising, the Convention Tax, and the Question of Linked Solutions

Two prominent bilateral trade issues to emerge during the past two years involve transactions that appear in the non-merchandise section of the current account, normally a quiet area in Canadian-American relations. These issues arose when each country discouraged transborder payments for a particular service that could be provided domestically. Although the two cases are unrelated, some Congressmen see linking them as the most logical way to resolve both — a proposal that is itself controversial.

---

[23] Instances of procurement preferences in the United States are listed in Canadian Export Association, *U.S. News*, June, 1978.

Canadian Discouragement of Cross-Border TV Advertising

The massive exposure of Canadians to the American way of life has made achieving an independent cultural identity a constant struggle for Canada. With respect to television broadcasting, one important expression of a national identity, the Canadian government has been trying in various ways to encourage more domestic programing. One handicap Canadian television networks have had to face in recent years is the financial drain that has been brought about by the growing practice of Canadian businesses to advertise on U.S. border stations. This practice has been made attractive by the widespread operation in Canada of cable TV systems that carry the signals of U.S. border stations and thereby give a large portion of the population the option of watching U.S. rather than Canadian programs.[24]

Following a 1971 policy statement by the Canadian Radio-Television Commission (CRTC), the Canadian government began considering two approaches to redirect Canadian advertising expenditures to Canadian stations. One was to require Canadian cable companies to delete commercials from imported U.S. programs, an idea that was never fully implemented and was finally withdrawn early in 1977. The second approach was to exclude tax deductions by Canadian business for TV advertising placed outside Canada. This measure was contained in Bill C-58, tax legislation enacted in 1976, and it has resulted in U.S. border stations losing up to half their advertising revenue from Canadian sources.[25]

Unlike some other bilateral trade issues arising from unilaterally imposed restrictions, the TV case does not lend itself to solution through compromise or compensation. Rather, it exemplifies those Canadian-U.S. issues where the injury being claimed in one country cannot be compared to the gains being sought in the other. This is especially true here, where the Canadian government's initiative serves greater cultural unity, an objective it considers non-negotiable.

The U.S. Convention Tax

The TV advertising issue might have remained modest and localized were it not for the simultaneous emergence of new regulations covering the attendance of Americans at foreign conventions.

A persistent theme of U.S. tax reform has been the need to close loopholes. The Tax Reform Act of 1976 (in force since the beginning

---

[24] Cable television is available to over 80 percent of Canadian households.

[25] The revenue from advertising directed primarily to markets in Canada for ten U.S. border stations fell from $18.9 million in 1975 to $9.2 million in 1977 ("Policies Affecting Services of United States Television Licensees," a submission by ten United States television licensees before the Trade Policy Staff Committee, February 13, 1978).

of 1977) includes provisions to curtail the practice of some Americans of writing off what amount to foreign vacations by deducting their expenses for attending conventions abroad. Specifically, Section 602 limits U.S. taxpayers' deductions to two conventions a year outside the United States, and for these it sets strict requirements on allowable expenses, attendance at meetings, and the paperwork to substantiate claims for deductions. The effect has been to divert the location of a number of conventions from foreign countries to the United States.

As frequently happens, a U.S. policy that treats the outside world as a whole has a particularly heavy impact on Canada. Because many organizations have both Canadian and U.S. members, they normally would hold some of their conventions in Canada; with this disincentive for U.S. members to meet outside the United States, however, there has been a large diversion of conventions from Canada. The total cost to Canada in lost revenue is estimated at $100-200 million annually.[26] This has added significantly to the already large deficit on the travel account, especially since the shift of jointly attended conventions from Canada to the United States involves both the loss of U.S. expenditures in Canada and greater Canadian expenditures south of the border. Canadians feel that the U.S. convention tax is unfair, given the logic for alternating convention locations between the two countries and the fact that Canadian tax law does not distinguish among the locations of meetings attended by its citizens.

This case, like that of Canadian TV advertising, involves injury in one country that cannot be measured against the goal originally sought in the other. Both the U.S. Administration and the Congress, which enacted Section 602, recognize the anomalies it has caused and have considered amendments.[27]

Issue Linking As an Issue

Congressional willingness to reconsider the convention tax appears to reflect in part the desire of some members to negotiate a deal with Canada involving compromises on its own TV advertising tax. The question of whether Section 602 and Bill C-58 should be

---

[26] See *Report by the Chairman of the House of Representatives Delegation to the Nineteenth Meeting of the Canada-United States Interparliamentary Group* (Washington, D.C.: U.S. Government Printing Office, 1978), p. 15.

[27] As part of his overall tax-reform package, President Carter proposed early in 1978 that most of the restrictions on tax deductions for travel to foreign conventions be eliminated when it is as reasonable to hold the convention outside the United States as within it because of the geographic composition of the membership or the purpose of the organization. Meanwhile, Congressman Rostenkowski introduced a bill that would exempt conventions held in North America from the restrictions of Section 602, while applying stricter reasonableness criteria than the President's proposal for convention travel outside North America.

linked for the purpose of resolving together the two bilateral problems they raise has come to generate considerable dissonance both within and between the governments.[28]

Generally speaking, U.S. Administration officials, their Canadian counterparts, and Canadian parliamentarians reject linkage of these two issues. They believe that, as a rule, Canadian-U.S. issues should be considered separately and on their merits unless some basic kinship exists. They see, however, no such natural linkage in kind or degree between either the goals of the two actions or their effects. Bill C-58 represents a major statement of Canadian national purpose, while Section 602 is part of a broad array of tax revisions which, when applied to Canada, are recognized as possibly creating as many inequities as they rectify. The financial losses resulting from the passage of Bill C-58 loom very large for a few U.S. broadcasting firms but total a fraction of those distributed more broadly in Canada by the convention tax.

Some U.S. Congressmen have developed a different perception — one shaped by the political process in which they participate. The strong constituency interests represented by a few border-state legislators are easily transmitted to other members, whereas the foreign government responsible for Bill C-58 has little opportunity to influence opinion. Given the parallel actions that would be required of the two legislative bodies to eliminate these problems — that is, restoration of recently removed tax exemptions for certain expenditures made in the other country — a trade-off seems naturally to suggest itself. The view by the U.S. delegation to the February, 1978, meeting of the Interparliamentary Group was that Bill C-58 and Section 602 "had become inexorably linked," a position that some Canadians regard as "congressional retaliation."[29]

It is too early to speculate, but if it turned out that the tendency of Congress to link these two issues — and perhaps others to come — prevailed over the U.S. Administration's preference to deal with them separately, this would represent a departure from the improved intergovernmental process of handling Canadian-American issues that has prevailed over the past two years.

Canada's Purchase of a New Fighter Aircraft

In accordance with its defence commitments to NATO and NORAD, Canada decided in 1977 to purchase 120-150 new jet fighters. With five of the six competing aircraft manufactured by U.S. companies (the sixth is made by a European consortium), the

[28]*Report of the Chairman* (op. cit., pp. 15-16) indicates this topic has sparked lively debate in meetings of the Interparliamentary Group.
[29]See, for example, Donald U. Alper and Robert L. Monahan, "Bill C-58 and the American Congress," *Canadian Public Policy*, Spring, 1978, pp. 184-92.

$2.3 billion that Canada expects to spend could mean this purchase will show up as a significant new element in bilateral trade.

Figuring prominently in Canada's choice of a plane will be the offsets Canada receives from the various bidders. The offsets can be expected to include not only a large share of the production of the aircraft in Canada, but also valuable transfers of technology and new export opportunities for Canadian businesses. For example, General Dynamics, one of the bidders, is reportedly offering to assign to Canada production of certain components of the aircraft wherever the market, as well as participation in other high-technology projects. Northrop, another bidder, offers a fourteen-year "export expansion program" to help diverse Canadian manufacturers find new markets abroad, plus a "new ventures program" designed to secure Canadian participation in advanced technology programs in which the company is involved.[30] When such programs include unrelated production, total offsets of over 100 percent are possible (say, 80 percent of the planes' value, plus an additional 30 percent of their value in other items to be made in Canada). The unrelated production could also increase Canadian exports to the United States to more nearly balance the bilateral trade effect of acquiring U.S. planes.

For $2.3 billion Canada will receive not only a fighter plane but also long-term benefits to its industrial structure and the development of skills. While Americans recognize procurement offsets to be a normal feature of defence-equipment exports, some are concerned that the level of benefits Canada may bargain for will lead to an unacceptably large diversion to Canada of what would otherwise be U.S. production and employment opportunities. The new fighter aircraft contract, therefore, has potentially important implications for Canada-U.S. trade relations.

---

[30] Details of the various bids can be found in *Globe and Mail* (Toronto), March 2, 1978; *Fortune*, April 10, 1978; and *Globe and Mail* (Toronto), June 10, 1978.

4

Bilateral Investment Patterns*

Canadian-American investment relationships have historically generated concern in Canada over the appropriateness of the magnitude of U.S. direct investment in Canada and, more recently, in the United States over the role of the Foreign Investment Review Agency (FIRA) in screening U.S. investment in Canada. During the past two years, however, these traditional concerns appear to have subsided. Rather, the fear has been increasingly expressed that various developments, especially those affecting costs, political uncertainties, and government policies, have reduced the incentives for direct investment in Canada to an extent that may be incompatible with Canadian aspirations for an ever-higher material standard of living. Moreover, unemployment problems, which are especially acute in some regions and industries, have turned the attention of governments at all levels in Canada to the task of attracting investment projects, regardless of ownership. One example is the offer of major incentives to encourage location of new automotive products plants in Canada, as discussed in Chapter 3.

Complicating this debate over investment relationships is the fact that both the economic environment and the economic policies pursued in the two countries have diverged significantly over the period 1976 to mid-1978. The purpose of this chapter is to identify the nature of some of the unusual shifts in the patterns of Canadian-U.S. investment transactions and to assess the extent that those have resulted from changing economic and political circumstances in the two countries. A fundamental question underlies this analysis. Have we witnessed the beginning of a major change that will affect investment patterns in the two countries in the long run, or can these changing patterns be explained by short-term variations in economic and political conditions in the two countries?

In some respects, when portfolio investment is considered, Canadians showed a greater dependency than usual on U.S. funds in the period under discussion. During 1976, for example, Canadian

---

* This chapter was prepared jointly by the staffs of the National Planning Association and the C. D. Howe Research Institute.

borrowers raised over $8.2 billion in long-term funds in U.S. capital markets, more than four times the average amount raised in the previous five years. The volume of bond financing then declined significantly in 1977, and that trend has continued in 1978, although the level of foreign debt financing remains high in relation to earlier years. However, there was evidence of a moderation in U.S. direct investment in Canadian industrial activity, as the additions to U.S. book value in Canada diminished and a number of U.S.-owned firms were repatriated to Canadian ownership. The 1976-77 period also witnessed very sharp fluctuations in the Canadian dollar. These fluctuations were both a response to trends in capital flows and a reflection of major shifts in Canada's economic situation.

While there has been talk in the past two years of the effects on capital flows and on the dollar of a shift in business confidence with respect to Canada, it is difficult to identify the impact of any such changes of attitude on the basis of available evidence from official statistics. Economic factors such as differences in the business cycle and in trends in interest rates provide plausible explanations for the shifts observed in investment patterns.

Bilateral investment flows are important to both countries. Canada receives the largest share of U.S. investment flows, and the United States is the largest foreign investor in Canada. Table 5 provides an overview of these investment flows since 1969, as shown by Canadian data. The first column shows that Canada built up an increasing deficit on current account (trade in goods and services) in the early 1970s. This deficit reached a peak of $4.8 billion in 1975 and has declined somewhat since then. The remaining columns show the trends in cross-border flows for direct investment, which gives the investor control over physical assets; in portfolio investment, which consists of purchases of public issues of bonds, debentures, and stocks; and in short-term capital flows, which include bank deposits and other investment instruments maturing in less than one year.

The following trends were apparent during the period covered in the table:

- Net inflows into Canada for direct investment by U.S. companies (column 2) have been fairly stable, with the exception of 1976, when there was a series of special transactions involving Canadian purchases of U.S.-owned facilities in Canada. Net outflows to the United States for direct investment by Canadians (column 3) have been higher in recent years than in the early 1970s.

- In portfolio transactions (column 4), net new Canadian issues in the United States soared to nearly $8.2 billion in 1976 and then declined sharply in 1977. Other portfolio transactions involving sales and purchases of outstanding securities (column 5) have normally produced an inflow of capital to Canada.

TABLE 5

Canada-U.S. Investment Flows,[a] **1969-77**
(million Canadian dollars)

Year	Current Account	Trans-Border Flows for Direct Investment		Portfolio Transactions		Long-Term Flows[b]	Short-Term Flows	Long-Term and Short-Term Flows
		United States in Canada	Canada in United States	Net New Canadian Issues	Other			
	(1)	(2)	(3)	(4)	(5)	(6)	(7)	(8)
1969	-845	564	-287	1,649	157	1,669	-239	1,430
1970	-165	628	-258	678	-115	989	47	1,036
1971	-86	599	-122	346	-42	877	1,867	2,744
1972	-137	457	-149	1,119	477	1,059	-201	858
1973	-834	423	-453	587	74	919	-590	329
1974	-1,530	615	-482	1,797	-25	1,572	1,660	3,232
1975	-4,810	564	-454	4,187	290	3,270	1,660	4,930
1976	-3,985	-490	-234	8,162	575	4,577	-351	4,226
1977	-3,934	516	-497	4,892	441	2,785	509	3,294

[a]This table is based on Canadian data. The official statistics issued by the two countries for these transactions are different and have not been reconciled (see Table 6, for example). A minus sign indicates a deficit in column 1 and capital outflows from Canada in the remaining columns.
[b]Includes long-term transactions for the Columbia River Treaty and export credit transactions by the Government of Canada.

Source: Statistics Canada, *Quarterly Estimates of the Canadian Balance of International Payments*, First Quarter, 1978 (Ottawa, 1978), Tables 3 and 16.

• Short-term capital flows have been erratic over the period, varying with the incentives created by interest-rate differentials between the two countries.

This chapter will describe the economic context affecting these transactions and then provide more detail on direct investment and on portfolio transactions.

The Economic Context

Chapter 2 includes a description of the differences in the patterns of economic performance in Canada and the United States in recent years. Basically, the United States has enjoyed a fairly strong and sustained economic expansion since the spring of 1975 — an expansion roughly similar to others of the postwar period, although not accompanied by as vigorous a recovery in business-capital spending. In contrast, Canada experienced a more moderate recession in 1975, which has been followed by a rather feeble economic recovery. Canada also exhibited a tendency toward significantly higher rates of price and wage increases during 1975 and 1976 — rates that led to a deterioration in the country's competitive position. As shown in Chart 2, in 1977 the rise in unit wage costs moderated as the Canadian dollar depreciated. This helped in eliminating much of the gap that had opened up in the previous years and left Canadian firms in a much more competitive position.[1]

During 1976, when cost differentials were at their widest, a number of other factors affected business confidence, including concern about the overall policy environment affecting business and, after November, 1976, the results of the provincial election in Quebec. These events reinforced the economic facts that seemed to favor direct investment in the United States.

The differences in the nature of the economic recovery in the two countries affected investment decisions in two ways. First, they influenced the market prospects for new direct investment. The steady increase in U.S. demand created better market opportunities than did the stagnating Canadian economy, thus creating an incentive for firms to invest in new plant facilities in the United States. Canada, in contrast, was just completing an investment boom,[2] with

---

[1] In 1977, unit labor costs in manufacturing (in U.S.-dollar terms) decreased by 1.8 percent in Canada and increased by 6.5 percent in the United States (Bureau of Labor Statistics, "International Comparisons of Productivity and Labor Costs in Manufacturing," *News*, May 12, 1978).

[2] For details of the investment picture, see Statistics Canada, *Public and Private Investment in Canada: Mid-Year Review*, 1978 (Ottawa, 1978). Canada enjoyed a strong investment surge from 1972 to 1975 and did not experience the sharp contraction in investment that hit the United States after the 1974-75 recession. During 1977 and the first six months of 1978, the volume of private investment spending in Canada did not increase significantly, but remained close to the high level established in the mid-1970s.

the result that there appeared to be sufficient capacity to meet prospective market demand.[3]

Second, the divergence in business cycles led to fairly substantial differences in monetary policies in the two countries in 1975 and 1976. Beginning in late 1975, the Bank of Canada began pursuing a more restrictive set of monetary policies; this has led to significantly higher interest rates in Canada than in the United States and, in turn, affected portfolio capital flows between the two countries. Chart 3 shows the trend in long-term interest rates since 1970. Rates are normally higher in Canada than in the United States, but in 1976 the gap between rates in the two countries was much wider than usual. This differential created a strong incentive for Canadian borrowers to seek funds in the United States. Chart 4 shows the

CHART 3

**Trends in Long-Term Interest Rates,
Canada and the United States, 1970-78**

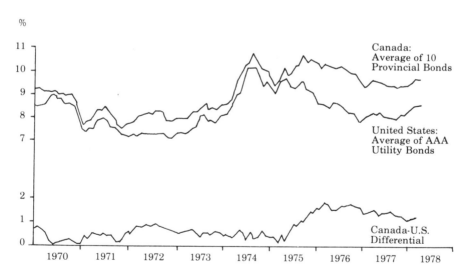

Source: *Bank of Canada Review*, April, 1978, p. 9.

---

[3] Indeed, Canada may be entering a period of relatively slow growth in housing and real estate activity as a result of changing demographic forces, especially the maturing of the baby-boom generation. Some forecasters anticipate an actual decline in the need for new housing units in the next five years. (See Earl D. Bederman [of the Canada Permanent Trust Co.], "Real Estate and Mortgage Markets in Canada: The Changing Context," speech given December 14, 1977.)

52

CHART 4

Trends in Short-Term Interest Rates, [a]
Canada and the United States, 1974-78

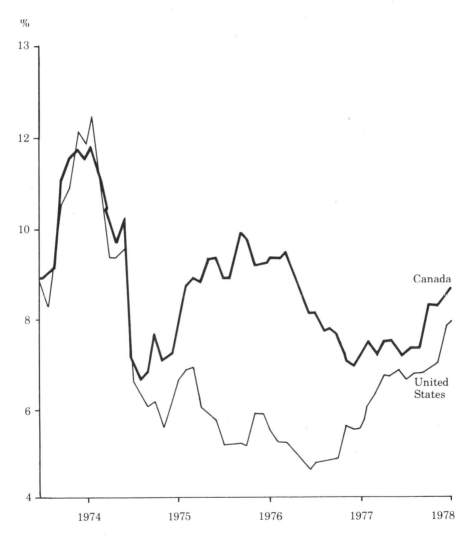

%

[a] Ninety-day finance company paper for Canada, and 90-day commercial paper for
the United States.

Source: Wood Gundy, *Fixed Income* (Toronto, various issues).

trends in short-term interest rates. Again, it is clear that Canadian
rates were significantly above the U.S. level — at times by as much
as 4 percentage points. Finally, Chart 5 shows the trend in the U.S.
price of the Canadian dollar. The Canadian dollar soared to a peak

of U.S.$1.039 in late 1976[4] before beginning a long depreciation. Its strength was generated by an inflow of long-term capital far in excess of the deficit in Canada's transactions in goods and services and seemed unsustainable to many observers concerned about the deterioration in the country's competitive costs and by the growing deficit on current account. Indeed, the general view at the time was that the Canadian dollar was overvalued, and this view inhibited the inflow of short-term capital and influenced the leads and lags in commercial foreign-exchange transactions.[5] As a result, the wide differential in short-term interest rates failed to attract a sustained inflow of capital.

CHART 5

Trends in Value of Canadian Dollar, 1970-78

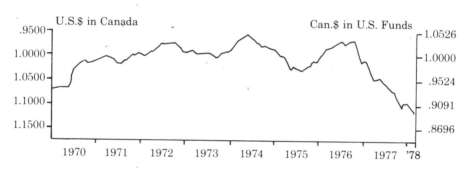

Source: *Bank of Canada Review*, April, 1978.

Trends in Direct Investment

The key determinants of changes in direct investment are relative yields on business opportunities and investors' assessments of market prospects.[6] Table 6 gives the official data published by the

---

[4] The peak in the monthly average was $1.039; the highest trading value was somewhat higher (Department of Finance, *Economic Review*, April, 1978 [Ottawa: Supply and Services Canada, 1978], p. 214).

[5] On this point see J. F. Dingle, "Major Developments in the Canadian Balance of Payments in 1976," *Bank of Canada Review*, April, 1977, p. 10.

[6] Whereas direct investment gives the foreign purchaser control over physical assets, portfolio investment is considered the purchase of public issues of bonds and debentures of governments and private corporations, as well as the purchase by individuals of stock in companies listed on Canadian, U.S., and other stock exchanges. At times the distinction between direct and portfolio investment is not entirely clear. For instance, it is conceivable that a large enough purchase of common shares (a portfolio transaction) could result in giving a U.S. buyer effective control of a Canadian firm (direct investment impact). In spite of this occasional overlapping, the broad determinants of each type of investment are still fundamentally quite distinct.

TABLE 6

U.S. Data on Flows Associated with U.S. Direct Investment in Canada, 1966-77[a]

(million U.S. dollars)

Year	(1) Net Outflows from U.S.[a]	(2) Reinvested Earnings	(3) Total Additions to Investment (1) + (2)	(4) Receipts of Income[b]	(5) Total Earnings (2) + (4)
1966	985	627	1,612	665	1,294
1967	372	650	1,022	691	1,341
1968	384	834	1,218	733	1,567
1969	582	1,002	1,584	641	1,643
1970	763	699	1,462	819	1,518
1971	64	1,023	1,087	848	1,871
1972	376	1,379	1,755	795	2,174
1973	581	1,867	2,448	977	2,844
1974	643	2,214	2,857	1,180	3,394
1975	419	2,173	2,592	1,239	3,412
1976	115	2,451	2,566	1,385	3,837
1977	-409	1,916	1,509	1,425	3,341

[a]Equity and intercompany accounts.
[b]Earnings remitted to the parent company in the form of dividends, interest, and so forth.

Sources: U.S. Department of Commerce, *Survey of Current Business* (Washington, D.C., 1977), August, 1977, pp. 42-43, and October, 1977, pp. 37-43. Data for 1976 and 1977 are preliminary estimates from *Survey of Current Business*, Part II, June, 1978, p. 39.

U.S. government on U.S. investment in Canada. Column 1 shows the actual cross-border flow of U.S. investment funds to Canadian affiliates.[7] Column 2 shows the earnings on existing Canadian operations that are reinvested in Canada. Column 3 shows total additions to the book value of U.S. investment in Canada. These additions to investment climbed quickly in the early 1970s, reaching a peak in 1974. Since then they have diminished, although the amount of new investment is still substantial.

The decline in the additions to investment seems to reflect at least two factors. First, there have been a number of Canadian takeovers of U.S.-owned firms in Canada. In 1976, for example, a number of U.S.-owned oil and potash firms and an aircraft firm were purchased by Canadians. (For a discussion of the potash takeovers, see Chapter 5.) Second, in 1977 there was a pronounced decline in the earnings of U.S.-owned firms in Canada (see column 5 of Table 6), and this reduced the amount of funds available for reinvestment in Canada. It remains to be seen, when the earnings improve in the future, whether there will be a corresponding pickup in the amount of reinvestment.

Another perspective on U.S. investment in Canada is provided in the reports of capital expenditures in Canada by U.S. companies. As shown in Table 7, these expenditures appear to follow the general trend of economic activity in Canada, rising when the economy is strong and weakening when activity in Canada slackens. For example, total expenditures declined modestly in 1967 and 1968, when there was a mild economic slowdown and a slump in total private investment in Canada. They then increased fairly steadily until 1974, declined in 1975, and increased at modest rates in 1976 and 1977. A December, 1977, survey by the U.S. Department of Commerce indicated that investment in 1978 would increase by only one percent, a revision downward from projections for 1978 first reported in June, 1977. This slow growth in planned expenditures in 1978 would certainly be consistent with the current rather sluggish pace of economic growth in Canada. However, a substantial amount of capital spending continues to take place.

Turning to Canadian direct investment in the United States, Table 8 shows that additions to book value (column 3) have followed

---

[7] The official Canadian data for U.S. direct investment in Canada show rather different patterns for the years 1976 and 1977. Officials at the U.S. Department of Commerce and at Statistics Canada have recently launched an effort to reconcile data on capital flows, but so far they have been unable to explain the divergence in the statistics. The sources of discrepancy include different criteria for foreign ownership, slightly different distinctions between direct and portfolio investment, and, most important, the inclusion in U.S. data of short-term transactions on intercompany accounts. In 1975 and 1976 the latter flows contributed −$153 million and +$216 million, respectively, to the U.S. figures given in Table 6.

TABLE 7

Capital Expenditures in Canada by U.S.-Affiliated Companies, 1967-78

Year	Expenditures (million $)	Percentage Change
Actual expenditures		
1967	2,400	−5
1968	2,300	−3
1969	2,600	14
1970	3,000	16
1971	3,500	16
1972	3,500	3
1973	4,200	21
1974	5,500	32
1975	5,000	−9
1976	5,600	10
Planned expenditures		
1977 (June, 1977)	6,000	7
1978 (June, 1977)	6,800	13
1977 (December, 1977)	5,900	5
1978 (December, 1977)	5,900	1

Sources: U.S. Department of Commerce, *Survey of Current Business, op. cit.*, March, 1975, p. 20, and March, 1978, p. 26.

TABLE 8

U.S. Data on Flows Associated with Canadian Investment in the United States, 1974-77
(million U.S. dollars)

Year	(1) Net Outflows from Canada[a]	(2) Reinvested Earnings	(3) Total Additions to Investment (1) + (2)	(4) Income Receipts	(5) Total Earnings (2) + (4)
1974	646	269	915	85	394
1975	−31	249	218	181	430
1976	313	247	560	232	479
1977	36	262	298	112	374

[a]Equity and intercompany accounts.

Sources: U.S. Department of Commerce, *Survey of Current Business, op. cit.*, October, 1977, pp. 37-43, and Part II, June, 1978, p. 39.

more of a seesaw pattern since 1974. In fact, the flow of Canadian direct investment into the United States reported here seems rather small in relation to the attention that has been paid to Canadian

investments in the U.S. market in recent years.[8] It is likely that some Canadian firms have been able to raise the capital invested in the United States from U.S. sources or by investing earnings on existing U.S. operations (see column 2 of Table 8). Under these circumstances the data on transborder transactions would understate Canadian interest in increased investments in the United States.

The difference in general economic conditions in the two countries in 1976 and 1977 probably tended to promote Canadian investment in the United States. As was explained earlier, the United States was launched on a significant economic expansion, creating market conditions that would tend to promote investment in new production capacity. Moreover, during 1976, when there was general alarm about the rise in unit labor costs in Canada, business quite naturally looked for lower-cost locations. Businesses making the decision to locate in the United States tended to cite both the desire to better serve the large U.S. market and the attraction of lower investment and operating costs.[9] There was also a good deal of comment about the tax incentives offered by some states in the South.[10] However, the surge in inflationary pressures in the United States in late 1977 and in 1978 and the recent improvement in Canada's cost situation suggest that some of the U.S. cost advantage has since been offset. It is therefore impossible to predict, at this stage, what the basic trend in Canadian investment in the United States is likely to be over the next few years. Official data do not confirm that the southbound flow of capital for direct investment purposes was unusually large in 1976 and 1977; moreover, some of the economic

---

[8] Examples over the past two years include "American Real Estate Attracting Canada," *Chicago Sun Times*, April 13, 1976; "West Canadians Scan U.S. for Plant Sites," *Christian Science Monitor*, September 8, 1976; "Alberta Companies Turn to U.S. for More Profitable Prospects," *Globe and Mail* (Toronto), October 1, 1976; "Canadian Real Estate Developers Shift Activities to U.S. Markets," *Journal of Commerce* (New York), November 10, 1976; "Ugly Canadians Buying up Western U.S. Resort Land," *Financial Post* (Toronto), October 23, 1977; "Unrest Spurs New Canadian Investment in Florida," *New York Times*, April 4, 1978.

[9] For example, senior executives of Atco Industries Limited in Calgary indicated a preference for U.S. locations to serve both the U.S. and export markets "because of their greater production efficiency and lower labor costs" (*Globe and Mail* [Toronto], July 24, 1976).

[10] See "Business Loves the Sunbelt, and Vice Versa," *Fortune*, June, 1977. Concern about the lure of the U.S. sunbelt for Canadian industry is expressed in *Canada Has a Future*, prepared for the Hudson Institute of Canada by Marie-Josée Drouin and B. Bruce-Briggs (Toronto: McClelland & Stewart, 1978), pp. 34-36. The Canadian report (Automotive Task Force, *Review of the North American Automotive Industry* [Ottawa: Department of Industry, Trade and Commerce, 1977]) notes that "a preliminary survey of the parts industry in Canada has confirmed that more and more competition is that of non-union plants located in the southern United States. One parts manufacturer indicated that his major competition was from a similar size plant located in Louisiana that had been given the land and service free, was experiencing a five year tax holiday, and enjoying a lower commercial interest rate on capital borrowed to construct the facility" (p. 172).

circumstances (such as relative costs) that might have promoted that southbound flow have since been altered.

In summary, the result of the southbound and northbound flows of capital in the period 1976-77 was that the combined net direct investment inflow into Canada was lower than in the 1960s and early 1970s, but this may have been due to a unique set of circumstances that were largely of a short-term nature.

Trends in Portfolio Investment

Portfolio investments generally represent either loans or scattered minority holdings of securities that do not give their owners control of a particular enterprise. Indeed, the initiative for portfolio borrowing has usually rested with the borrower, not the foreign lender. The present high degree of financial integration between Canada and the United States has, to a great extent, been achieved through the growth in the volume and frequency of portfolio capital movements across the border. On several counts the Canadian-U.S. borrower-lender relationship is unique. Close links have been forged between the two capital markets, and the flows between them have shown a tremendous responsiveness to economic and political developments in both countries. The magnitude of these portfolio flows has created one of the largest borrower-lender relationships in the world.[11]

Table 9 provides an overview of trends in Canada's long-term borrowing in other countries in recent years. During the period covered in the table, there were two notable shifts in Canada's long-term borrowing activity. First, the total value of foreign borrowing increased dramatically in 1976 and remained rather high in 1977. Thus Canada appears to be making a shift toward greater use of foreign-debt capital than of equity capital, with the result that there is a tendency to maintain greater ownership and control of new investment activity. Second, as will be shown below, both public and private borrowers in Canada have begun to turn to European and other capital markets to supplement their traditional borrowing in New York.

The flood of foreign bond issues by Canadians in 1976 reflects the coincidence of at least three factors:

- The unusually wide interest-rate differentials described earlier, which encouraged Canadian borrowers to seek foreign funds.

---

[11] For a detailed examination of the operation of North American capital markets, see the forthcoming study by Robert M. Dunn, Jr., entitled *The Canada-U.S. Capital Market: Intermediation, Integration, and Policy Independence*, sponsored jointly by the C. D. Howe Research Institute and the National Planning Association.

TABLE 9

**Net New Security Issues[a] Abroad by
Canadian Borrowers, 1971-77**
(million Canadian dollars)

	1971	1972	1973	1974	1975	1976	1977
Government of Canada	−2	−2	−90	−45	−37	−2	−2
Provinces and provincial agencies	400	847	526	1,487	2,893	4,376	2,589
Municipalities	−51	72	29	160	479	699	280
Corporations:							
Bonds	30	69	−24	241	606	2,905	2,138
Stocks	11	12	51	17	16	65	—
Short-term paper	−23	−7	55	69	251	331	72
Total	370	990	509	1,921	4,208	8,373	5,077

[a]Includes U.S.-dollar issues and Canadian-dollar issues placed in overseas markets.

Source: *Bank of Canada Review*, June, 1978, Table 30.

- The unusually high level of provincial-government and provincial crown-corporation capital requirements in 1976. These capital requirements, in turn, were the result of three factors:
  - High provincial deficits, reflecting rapid spending growth and slow revenue growth in the aftermath of the recession. These deficits have since been reduced considerably as a result of expenditure control and tax increases.
  - Special financing by Quebec to help cover the deficit for the 1976 Olympic Games and also for advance funding by Hydro-Québec (which subsequently borrowed less than usual in 1977).
  - High capital requirements for provincial utilities launched on ambitious hydro-electric and nuclear programs. Ontario, Manitoba, and British Columbia have since stretched out their construction plans as a result of revised forecasts showing slower growth in energy demand in the 1980s, but these capital requirements will remain substantial in future years.
- Removal of the withholding tax on interest payments on corporate bonds, eliminating a major obstacle to corporate issues abroad. (Note in Table 9 the surge in corporate issues that resulted in 1976 and 1977.)

By 1977 some of the forces promoting foreign borrowing began to reverse. Specifically, interest-rate differentials between Canada and the United States narrowed during 1977, as interest rates increased in the United States and short-term interest rates declined sharply in Canada (see Charts 3 and 4). This reduced the incentive to borrow abroad. At the same time, the volume of provincial financing

tended to diminish as the provinces introduced stricter budgetary controls. The impact of these changes is reflected in Table 10. The value of all foreign-security issues dropped sharply in 1977, although the decline was much more significant for U.S.-dollar issues than for issues in other currencies. At the same time the volume of domestic financing soared, from $12 billion in 1976 to $19 billion in 1977, with the result that foreign securities provided 40 percent of new financing for Canadian borrowers in 1976 and only 21 percent in 1977.

One of the most significant recent trends in capital-market flows reflected in this table is Canada's growing use of capital markets in Europe and Japan. Indeed, a sizable trading volume of Euro-Canadian issues has begun to develop as Canadian borrowers have attempted to diversify their foreign sources of funds by exploiting these new markets.

TABLE 10

Canadian Domestic and Foreign Net New Issues,[a] **1971-77**
(million Canadian dollars)

Type of Issue	1971	1972	1973	1974	1975	1976	1977
Foreign:							
U.S. dollars	204	526	562	1,458	2,911	5,275	2,619
Other currencies	166	464	−53	463	1,297	3,097	2,458
	370	990	509	1,921	4,208	8,372	5,077
Domestic	7,585	6,523	5,382	12,011	12,121	12,400	19,004
Total net new issues	7,955	7,513	5,891	13,932	16,329	20,773	24,081
U.S.-dollar issues as percentage of total	2.6	7.0	9.5	10.5	17.8	25.4	10.9
Other currency issues as percentage of total	2.0	6.2	−0.9	3.3	8.0	14.9	10.2
Foreign issues as percentage of total	4.6	13.2	8.6	13.8	25.8	40.3	21.1

[a]Includes short-term paper, bonds and stocks, Canada Savings Bonds, and Canada Pension Plan. Bank loans are not included.

Source: *Bank of Canada Review*, June, 1978, Table 28.

This surge of foreign borrowing in the United States and abroad in the mid-1970s will have an impact on Canada's balance of international transactions for some years to come. First, interest payments on this new debt will add considerably to the deficit on service transactions (see Table 3). Second, since most of this debt is denominated in foreign currencies,[12] Canadians will bear the risks

---

[12]Canadian issues in the New York market are almost always denominated in U.S.

associated with possible foreign-exchange movements. Any depreciation in the Canadian dollar will mean higher effective interest costs
and higher repayments of capital in terms of Canadian dollars (and,
of course, any appreciation will lighten these costs). This effect was
noticeable in early 1978, when the value of the Canadian dollar declined sharply, leading to an increase in the deficit on interest
transactions with other countries.

The data do not present a particularly dramatic story of fundamental shifts in bilateral transactions in 1976 and 1977. There have
definitely been some wide swings in both direct and portfolio flows,
and there are certainly some contradictions in the official statistics
published in the two countries. But the data do not reflect an abrupt
change in foreign investors' confidence in Canada, despite allega-
tions of a massive outflow of capital from Canada as a result of an
unfriendly investment climate.[13] Although the importance of business confidence cannot be overlooked, interest-rate differentials and
variations in market prospects appear to explain many of the shifts
that occurred.

However, it is important to note that flows of short-term capital
did not respond to interest-rate spreads in the way that might have
been expected. In 1976, in particular, although short-term interest
rates favored capital inflows, there was, in fact, a small net outflow
(a large outflow in the third quarter and a large inflow in the fourth
quarter). Moreover, Statistics Canada has reported an increase in
unaccounted-for capital flows in the balance of payments accounts.
This item, formerly called the balancing item, has generally been
negative over the years, indicating an outflow of funds; but in the
past two years it has increased sharply, from an average of $830
million during the period 1970-75 to $3.5 billion in 1976 and $2.4
billion in 1977.[14] This increase in the balancing item (now called er-
rors and omissions) suggests that fairly large outflows of funds have
not been recorded through official reporting channels.[15]

----

dollars, but a sizable portion of those issued in Europe are denominated in Canadian dollars.

[13] See articles cited in footnote 8.

[14] Statistics Canada, *Quarterly Estimates of the Canadian Balance of International
Payments*, First Quarter, 1978 (Ottawa, 1978). The unaccounted-for items amounted
to 2.2 percent of gross flows of international payments in 1976, compared to 1.4 percent in 1972 and 1977, suggesting that, while the item is large in absolute terms, it
may not be out of proportion with past experience.

[15] Statistics Canada collects regular reports on bank deposits and on corporate transactions, but it is unable to collect reports on transactions of individuals buying real
estate for their own use.

[16] Bank of Canada, *Annual Report of the Governor to the Minister of Finance*, 1976
(Ottawa, 1977), p. 9; and Judith Maxwell, *Policy Review and Outlook, 1977: An
Agenda for Change* (Montreal: C. D. Howe Research Institute, 1977), Chap. 3, "Bal-
ance of Payments Concerns and Constraints." For an American perspective on this
question, see Richard Schmeelk (General Partner, Salomon Brothers), speech to The
Conference Board in Canada, Toronto, June 27, 1978.

Summary

During the 1976-77 period many questions were raised about Canada's economic and political future and increasing dependence on foreign capital to finance government deficits and to balance the large deficit on current account. Canadians themselves have been discussing the implications of this borrowing,[16] and governments and their agencies have begun to make serious efforts to scale down their borrowing to the level required to finance the deficit on current account. Indeed, provincial and corporate borrowing subsided so quickly in the winter of 1978 that there was a temporary vacuum in portfolio transactions that contributed to an abrupt decline in the value of the dollar. Consequently, the federal government decided to issue $750 million in securities in New York in order to fill the gap.[17]

During the latter part of 1977 and early 1978, economic trends in Canada and the United States continued to diverge, but this time on somewhat different courses. Renewed inflationary pressures began to emerge in the United States, while the increase in production costs continued to moderate in Canada. The combination of the two has led to a more favorable cost position for Canadian firms than prevailed in the period under discussion. It is much too early to suggest that the unusual shifts in investment patterns in 1976-77 herald a new era in the Canadian-American relationship. What is clear, however, is that investment transactions between the countries continue to promote a highly integrated North American capital market and that integration will continue to have important repercussions both for economic policy in Canada and for investors on either side of the border.

---

[17]For a description of this aspect of federal economic policy, see George Freeman, speech to the Canadian Association for Business Economics, reprinted in *Bank of Canada Review*, May, 1978.

5

Energy Relations and Other Resource Issues*

Trade in natural resources is one of the most important linkages between the economies of Canada and the United States. The United States relies on Canada as a secure source for many of the raw materials for which its domestic production is less than its requirements. The Canadian economy is geared heavily toward the export of natural-resource products, with the United States being by far the largest market.

Most recently, energy has dominated resource issues between the two countries, just as it has dominated resource issues throughout the world. Two events have been particularly significant in bilateral energy relations in the past two years: the implementation of the Canadian decision, announced in 1974, to phase out crude-oil exports to the United States and the negotiation of an agreement to build a pipeline to transport Alaskan natural gas through Canada to markets in the Lower 48 states. The first two sections of this chapter examine the circumstances surrounding these events. The third section reviews a number of other recent bilateral developments on the energy front — including plans for strategic oil storage, the possibility of liquified-natural-gas exports from Canada to the United States, emergency sharing of energy supplies, and trade patterns in coal and uranium between the two countries.

The final section of this chapter examines a number of other questions involving resource use and the operations of resource industries that have either emerged or taken on new significance in the past two years. The issues range from transnational government involvement in particular industries, to use of resources in the oceans where clear claims to ownership have not been established, to cross-border environmental concerns. While, individually, they do not rank in importance with the energy issues, collectively they have the potential for making a major impact on the nature of Canada-U.S. relations.

---

* This chapter was prepared by Richard Shaffner, a member of the staff of the C. D. Howe Research Institute.

The Phaseout of Canadian Oil Exports

Canada and the United States face quite similar problems in terms of their most important energy source — oil. Both must import oil to meet domestic demand; and while both have considerable reserves in non-conventional deposits such as the Colorado oil shales and the Alberta oilsands and anticipate possible large conventional oil-reserve increases through discoveries offshore and in the Arctic and through improvements in recovery technology, the consensus is that it will not be possible to develop these resources quickly enough to compensate for the decline in production from existing areas and the anticipated increase in demand. The National Energy Board (NEB) has estimated that by 1985 Canada will be importing 1.2 million barrels per day of crude petroleum and equivalent (compared to 0.7 million barrels per day in 1977), while Canadian production will be only 1.0 million barrels per day.[1] The Federal Energy Administration, meanwhile, has forecast that in 1985 the United States will need to import 12-16 million barrels of oil per day (compared to 8 million in 1977) to supplement the expected 9-11 million barrels per day of domestic production.[2]

Only a few years ago it was not anticipated that Canada would be a net importer of oil in the late 1970s. During the 1960s and early 1970s Canadian oil production grew steadily, and Canadian exports became an important source of oil to the United States.[3] In 1972 Canada supplied 39 percent of imported crude oil to the United States, making it the single most important foreign supplier. In February, 1973, Canada put controls on its crude-oil exports to preserve sufficient supplies for domestic requirements in the face of burgeoning U.S. demand, but it was still widely anticipated that Canada would be able to sustain considerable exports for a number of years. A report of the Department of Energy, Mines and Resources released in 1973, for example, indicated the possibility of Canada's providing up to 10 percent of U.S. oil demand in 1985, compared with 6 percent in 1972.[4]

---

[1] National Energy Board, *Canadian Oil: Supply and Requirements*, February, 1977 (Ottawa, 1977), p. 85. The figures cited are those the NEB expects are most likely. The NEB is careful to point out that there are many variables involved and that, using different assumptions, the deficiency of supply relative to requirements could be anywhere from .8 to 1.8 million barrels per day.

[2] Executive Office of the President, Energy Policy and Planning, *The National Energy Plan* (Washington, D.C.: U.S. Government Printing Office, 1977), pp. 11 and 14.

[3] Canadian exports of crude oil to the United States grew from 465 thousand barrels per day in 1968 to an all-time high of 1.1 million barrels per day in 1973. Canada was able to export significant quantities of oil because its domestic market was divided so that all requirements east of a line along the Ottawa Valley were supplied by imports. Until 1972 Canada was a net importer of oil, since exports from Canada's western oil-producing regions were less than imports into the area east of the Ottawa Valley. (Data from *Oilweek*, February 13, 1978.)

[4] Department of Energy, Mines and Resources, *An Energy Policy for Canada: Phase I*, Vol. I (Ottawa: Information Canada, 1973), p. 127.

In late 1974, however, the Canadian government announced it would be phasing out crude-oil exports by the early 1980s. This decision reflected both the realization that Canada's productive capacity from conventional sources had peaked and the desire to reduce dependence on foreign sources of supply, which had been shown to be less certain by the Arab oil embargo and which had increased sharply in price.[5] The decision caused a considerable jolt to Canada-U.S. energy relations; the United States was particularly upset that there had been so little prior consultation.[6] It also added to the irritation in the United States generated by Canada's decision, in September, 1973, to impose a tax on each barrel of exported oil to make the price received equal to the cost of imported oil into Montreal.[7]

Since 1975 there has been evidence that the tension created by Canada's oil-export policies has eased. In September, 1975, the National Energy Board provided estimates of the level of permissible exports for each year to 1982, as well as a formula by which these could be calculated.[8] The NEB indicated that one reason it was doing this was to help U.S. users of Canadian crude plan for alternate sources of supply. The NEB provided further information of assistance to U.S. users when, in a report released in February, 1977, it broke allowable exports down into light and heavy crude oil.[9] Finally, there now seems to be a more general acceptance in the United States of the fact that the Canadian decision represents a justifiable position. For example, Frank G. Zarb, when administrator of the Federal Energy Administration, stated before the Joint Economic Committee of the U.S. Congress that, in their phasing out of oil exports, "Canadians have set themselves a very reasonable national goal, one that I would use if I were laying out their particular program."[10]

---

[5] Exports were reduced by the Canadian government's decision to shut in some of Canada's productive capacity in order to stretch out the life of existing reserves in the 1980s. In addition, it was decided to extend the Canadian pipeline system to Montreal so that Canadian oil would be able to supply 250,000 barrels per day of domestic demand in the area east of the Ottawa Valley, which until that time had been supplied by imported oil. This meant that Canadian oil previously available for export became directed to the domestic market.

[6] For more detail see Canadian-American Committee, *A Time of Difficult Transitions: Canada-U.S. Relations in 1976* (Montreal and Washington, 1976), pp. 46-47.

[7] The tax brought the export price of Canadian oil up to approximately the OPEC price. The tax revenue was used to subsidize consumers in Eastern Canada, who had to rely on imports for their oil supplies and consequently were suddenly confronted with the much higher world oil prices.

[8] National Energy Board, *Canadian Oil: Supply and Requirements*, September, 1975 (Ottawa, 1975), pp. 44-47.

[9] National Energy Board, *Canadian Oil*, February, 1977, *op. cit.*, pp. 70-73.

[10] Congress of the United States, Joint Economic Committee, *Canadian Oil Policies and Northern Tier Energy Alternatives* (Washington, D.C.: U.S. Government Printing Office, 1977), p. 8.

With the exception of heavy crudes, for which the market is very limited, the evidence is heavily weighted against any reversal of Canada's position on oil exports. The NEB expects that, by about 1981, production of Canadian crude oil and equivalent will fall below the requirements of the domestic market presently supplied by Canadian crude (that is, west of the Ottawa Valley plus 250 thousand barrels per day east of the Ottawa Valley) and that by 1985 there will be a deficiency from Canadian production in this market of about 450 thousand barrels per day.[11] The NEB expects that the impact of additions to established reserves in conventional areas and of improved recovery technology will fall well short of compensating for the anticipated reduction in production from established crude reserves.[12] Moreover, it seems most unlikely that the volume of frontier oil that could be made available to Canadian markets by 1985 would be large enough to have very much impact on the NEB's calculations. Finally, while the oil sands have great potential for increasing Canada's crude-oil production in the longer run, the NEB believes that economic conditions and financial-feasibility problems will preclude a third project's coming into operation before 1987, and a fourth's before 1991. (The Great Canadian Oil Sands mine has been in operation since 1967, and the Syncrude project came on stream during 1978.) In the case of heavy crudes, the NEB has decided Canada's export position should be determined independently of other crudes. Heavy crude differs significantly from light crude in use and refining characteristics and in that there are proportionately greater prospects for increasing current levels of production in Canada. Consequently, the NEB projects that Canada will have a small exportable surplus of heavy crude until about 1991.[13]

Canadian crude-oil exports to the United States have been mainly to refineries in the so-called Northern Tier states (Michigan, Wisconsin, Minnesota, North Dakota, Montana, and Washington). The phasing out of Canadian supplies creates a dual problem for the Northern Tier; in the long run a transportation system must be developed to supply crude from other sources to refineries formerly fed by pipelines from Western Canada; in the short run an interim means of supplying their petroleum needs must be organized. Both questions have major implications for Canada-U.S. energy relations.

---

[11] National Energy Board, *Canadian Oil*, February, 1977, *op. cit.*, p. 84.

[12] There has been a significant revival in exploration activity in Alberta and British Columbia recently, one result of which has been the discovery of what is considered the best oil find in Western Canada in a decade — West Pembina. The exploration effort does not appear to be sufficiently successful, however, to turn around the overall picture of declining reserves.

[13] National Energy Board, *Canadian Oil*, February, 1977, *op. cit.*, p. 72. These calculations exclude the possible effects of heavy-oil upgrading, which would transfer some oil from the heavy-oil category to the light-oil category. Several proposals have been made for building heavy-oil upgrading facilities.

Oil Exchanges

To ease the short-run problem, the Federal Energy Administration (FEA) implemented on January 1, 1976, a Canadian crude-oil-allocation program to assure the refineries most seriously affected by the cutback in Canadian supplies priority in what was available. Through increased utilization of existing crude and product pipelines by areas adjacent to the Northern Tier and through the expansion of a crude-oil pipeline from Iowa into the Minneapolis area, the FEA anticipates that only Montana and eastern Washington will actually experience supply shortages in the period to 1980, although a number of refineries in other Northern Tier states will be forced to operate well below capacity.[14] One way that both the actual shortages and the refinery-undercapacity problem could be eased during the interim period would be for oil companies in Canada and the United States to make exchanges on a no-net-export basis. Discussions to permit such swaps were initiated by the U.S. State Department and the FEA in 1975, and exchanges began taking place on a small scale in 1976. By late 1977 roughly 60,000 barrels per day of Western Canadian crude were going to the Northern Tier states in exchange for an equal amount of U.S. oil coming into the Ontario and Quebec markets.

Canada initially took the position that it did not want the oil exchanges to increase its dependence on imported oil; hence it was only willing to accept oil of U.S. domestic origin. This meant that exchanges probably could not have expanded much beyond 60,000 barrels per day because of the problems of getting U.S. oil into Canada; there is limited pipeline capacity for direct movements northward across the border, and moving U.S. crude from Gulf ports by tanker to Montreal is hampered by the extra transportation costs of $1.00-2.00 per barrel and by a shortage of loading facilities at Gulf ports. The Canadian government opened the door for larger oil swaps when it eased this logistics problem for Canadian and U.S. oil companies by removing its restrictions on the use of foreign oil in December, 1977, having concluded that doing so did not pose a threat to Canada's oil-supply security. This conclusion reflected the view that if, during an emergency, the flow of foreign oil coming into Canada on a swap basis were interrupted, Canadians could stop their deliveries to the United States. Despite the removal of this limitation, however, oil exchanges in the first three months of 1978 increased only slightly, to about 80,000 barrels per day, one reason being that the potential for exchanges is limited by the Canadian government's policy that 250,000 barrels of Western Canadian crude oil per day must be supplied to the Montreal-area market. If part of this flow were directed to the U.S. Northern Tier market, and

---

[14]Federal Energy Administration, "Petroleum Supply Alternatives for the Northern Tier States Through 1980," mimeographed, June, 1977.

foreign oil supplied in exchange to the Montreal market, the scope for swaps would be immediately increased.

Moving Alaskan Oil to the Northern Tier States

The solution to the long-run oil-supply problem of the Northern Tier states would appear to be the replacement of Canadian crude with that recently available from Alaska's North Slope. Several proposals have been, or are currently, under consideration for moving Alaskan crude to markets in the interior of the continental United States:[15]

- A "Northern Tier" pipeline would be built from a tanker terminal at Port Angeles, Washington, across the northern states to Minnesota.

- A pipeline would be built from a tanker terminal at Kitimat, British Columbia, to Edmonton, Alberta, where it would link up with the pipeline system that was delivering Canadian crude to the Northern Tier before the phaseout of Canadian exports.

- Port facilities at Cherry Point, Washington, would be expanded, and by reversing the flow of the Trans Mountain Pipeline between Edmonton and Vancouver, crude would be moved to Edmonton, where it would be placed in the existing pipelines connecting with the Northern Tier.

- Crude would be landed at Long Beach, California, and sent through a converted natural gas pipeline to Midland, Texas, where it would be refined and put in product pipelines for the northern states.

- A pipeline would be built along the same route as the Alaska Highway natural gas pipeline (discussed in the next section), linking the Trans-Alaska pipeline at Fairbanks to existing pipeline systems in Edmonton, Alberta.

For environmental and other reasons, all these proposals face obstacles to their approval; the prospects for two of the three proposals with bilateral implications are bleak. The scheme to reverse the Trans Mountain Pipeline was effectively killed in October, 1977, by an amendment to the U.S. Marine Mammal Protection Act, which will prevent expansion of the Cherry Point terminal. In addition, the Canadian government indicated in February, 1978, that it would be interested in seeing the Kitimat proposal proceed only if Canada needed it for itself.[16] The Kitimat scheme has attracted much interest in the United States because it would require only about 750

---

[15] Because Alaskan crude has a higher sulphur content than Western Canadian crude, it will not be a ready substitute for Canadian crude in all Northern Tier refineries. This may mean some costly redesigning of certain refineries. Alternately, "sweet" imported crude may have to be mixed with "sour" Alaskan crude to make the feedstock more suitable for refineries as presently designed.

[16] This position was indicated by Prime Minister Trudeau as being the consensus of

miles of new pipeline construction (considerably less than the Northern Tier pipeline); it would involve a shorter sea link with Valdez, Alaska; and it could be expected to encounter less resistance on environmental grounds (in the United States) than the others. In October, 1977, for example, the U.S. House of Representatives Sub-committee on Energy and Environment passed a resolution request-ing that the President initiate talks with Canadian authorities on the project. While Canadian officials recognize that the Kitimat pipeline could ultimately increase Canada's flexibility in obtaining imports from foreign sources such as Indonesia, there has been vocal opposition to the proposal by local fishermen operating on the Pacific coast and by environmentalists generally, and it appears that, for political reasons, the Canadian government does not want to risk serious oil-transportation mishaps when the proposal is only for moving U.S. oil to U.S. markets.

Consideration of the third possibility with bilateral implications, an Alaska Highway oil pipeline, is at a very preliminary stage. It is generally conceded that construction could not begin until comple-tion of the gas pipeline.

The Alaska Highway Natural Gas Pipeline

As in the case of oil, Canada for many years has been an impor-tant source of natural gas for the United States. While imports from Canada, which averaged 990 billion cubic feet per year in the period 1972-75, were only 4.7 percent of total U.S. gas demand, they made up a large share of the market in some parts of the Midwest and on the west coast.[17] In 1975 the prospects for Canada's conventional gas reserves seemed to resemble those for its oil reserves, and it looked as though Canada would be unable to meet both its domestic and its export commitments.[18] Since Canada's exports of gas involved long-term contracts with U.S. customers (which is not the case for oil ex-ports, where permits are for only thirty days), it appeared that rec-onciling how the shortages would be shared would be a critical test for Canada-U.S. relations.[19]

The fear of a curtailment of Canadian exports to the United States now seems to have been premature. Increases in the price of

---

his Cabinet (*Globe and Mail* [Toronto], February 24, 1978). In a technical sense the Kitimat project was given a serious setback when the NEB announced a short time before that it would not be able to take up the Kitimat proposal before the fall of 1978, when it had completed a special national oil-dependency study.

[17] U.S. Department of the Interior, Bureau of Mines, *Commodity Data Summaries*, 1977, p. 108.

[18] A National Energy Board report released in 1975 concluded that conventional pro-ducing areas would not be able to satisfy Canada's domestic requirements beyond 1984 even if all exports were cut off (National Energy Board, *Canadian Natural Gas: Supply and Requirements*, April, 1975, pp. 68-69).

[19] For more background on this threat to relations, see Canadian-American Commit-tee, *op. cit.*, pp. 47-50.

gas in Canada to make it more closely resemble the price of oil gave a powerful stimulus to gas exploration in Canada's conventional gas-producing areas of Alberta and British Columbia. The result has been a large increase in reserves in these areas and a surplus in productive capacity that has been estimated at 400 billion cubic feet for 1977 and 1978, or about 25 percent of actual production.[20] At the same time, domestic demand for gas has been retarded by the price increase.[21] As a consequence, attention has now turned to the possibilities of either accelerating delivery of export commitments to the United States or making increased commitments, rather than cutting them back.

Since the first hydrocarbon reserves were located on Alaska's North Slope in the winter of 1967/68, both Canada and the United States have discovered substantial natural gas deposits in the Arctic region. The Prudhoe Bay field contains over 26 trillion cubic feet of salable natural gas, and the Mackenzie Delta-Beaufort Sea fields are officially estimated to contain over 5 trillion cubic feet, although recent exploration has identified additional large reserves.[22] The major achievement in Canada-U.S. energy relations in the past two years was the successful negotiation of an agreement facilitating the construction of a pipeline system to move this gas to southern markets.[23]

The route chosen was the Alaska Highway, or Alcan route, which initially will involve building a pipeline from Prudhoe Bay across Alaska, the southern Yukon, northern British Columbia, and Alberta, where it will split into two legs, one ending in northern California and the other in Illinois (see Map 1). Subsequently, it will be possible to build a spur to this pipeline from Whitehorse to connect to Canadian natural gas in the Mackenzie Delta and the Beaufort Sea. Because of its less harmful social and environmental impact, the Alaska Highway route won out over another joint route,

---

[20] National Energy Board, *Reasons for Decision: Northern Pipelines* (Ottawa: Supply and Services Canada, 1977), p. 1-81.

[21] In addition, in the industrial market, natural gas competes with residual petroleum products. The prices of all oil products have gone up, and demand has been below projections, but the demand for residual oil has been weaker than for gasoline and light fuel oil because there are more readily available substitutes, such as natural gas and electricity, and because the industrial sector has been the quickest to respond to energy-saving measures. To preserve as much of a market as possible, there has been considerable price discounting in residual petroleum products by oil refiners.

[22] National Energy Board, *Reasons for Decision, op. cit.*, pp. 2-130 and 2-168. Dome Petroleum Ltd. of Calgary is reported to be exploring a natural gas zone that it estimates could contain as much as 20 trillion cubic feet of gas (*Gazette* [Montreal], September 23, 1977).

[23] The agreement was signed on September 20, 1977, by the U.S. Secretary of Energy, James R. Schlesinger, and the Canadian Deputy Prime Minister, Allan J. MacEachen, the two men who headed the negotiations. It was given final congressional approval in the United States on November 2, and the necessary enabling legislation was signed into law in Canada on April 12, 1978.

MAP 1

Route of the Alaska Highway Natural Gas Pipeline

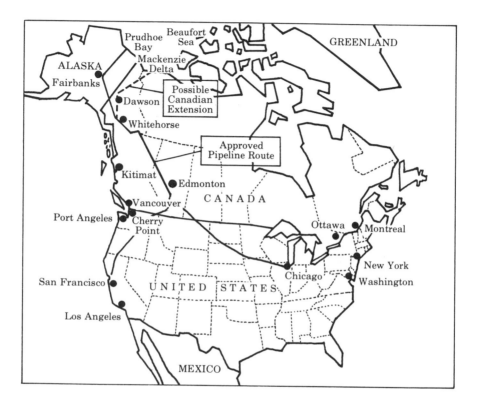

one that would have gone from Prudhoe Bay east along the coast of the Beaufort Sea and up the Mackenzie River Valley to Alberta.[24] Either country could have chosen a natural gas transportation system that would have been independent of the other country, but both opted for the joint project. Canada rejected an all-Canadian pipeline, one that would have connected the Mackenzie Delta to

---

[24]Canada rejected the Mackenzie Valley alternative after the Mackenzie Valley Pipeline Inquiry, headed by Mr. Justice Thomas Berger, concluded that, for environmental reasons, a pipeline should not be built across the northern Yukon and that any pipeline construction in the Mackenzie Valley should be delayed for ten years to permit time for native claims to be settled and for new programs and new institutions to be established to diminish its social impact (Report of the Mackenzie Valley Pipeline Inquiry, *Northern Frontier, Northern Homeland* [Ottawa: Supply and Services Canada, 1977]). The National Energy Board accepted the Berger Inquiry's conclusions in its decision in favor of the Alaska Highway route (NEB, *Reasons for Decision, op. cit.*).

Alberta via the Mackenzie River Valley, because insufficient reserves had been proved in the Delta region to make the necessary investment viable. The United States chose the route through Canada because it would ultimately deliver Prudhoe Bay gas at a lower cost to the U.S. consumer than the alternative — moving it by pipeline to the south coast of Alaska and shipping it as liquified natural gas (LNG) to California.

The environment for a joint project was enhanced by the establishment of a transit pipeline treaty between Canada and the United States. Negotiations on the treaty were initiated in 1974, it was signed on January 28, 1977, and it entered into force on September 19, 1977. The treaty provides for unimpeded transmission of hydrocarbons and for non-discriminatory treatment with regard to taxes and other monetary charges for all existing and future pipelines in the two countries for thirty-five years. While the two countries have had a long history of successful bilateral cooperation on pipelines, this treaty served to further allay any misgivings about the dangers of a joint project.

Negotiating the Pipeline Agreement

Estimates of the cost of the Alaska Highway natural gas pipeline range upward from $10.3 billion.[25] In a project of this size there is inevitably much concern about the ultimate direct and indirect costs and benefits to the two countries, evaluations of which are influenced by different national objectives: the United States is mainly interested in getting its Alaskan natural gas to markets at the lowest possible cost to the consumer, while Canada is interested in maximizing the benefits from construction in terms of employment and materials contracts and in minimizing the social dislocations and the environmental impact that may result. (Until a decision is made to link up the Mackenzie Delta gas, virtually all the gas flowing through the pipeline will be destined for markets in the United States.)

Some of the concerns over the costs and benefits figured prominently in the bilateral negotiations. For example, Canada wanted the pipeline to swing to the north of the Alaska Highway in the Yukon to pass through Dawson, so that, when the link with the Mackenzie Delta was built, the cost would be smaller. The United States preferred the southern route along the Alaska Highway through Whitehorse because it would be cheaper, a saving that would be reflected in the price of Alaskan gas to consumers. The compromise reached was to build the southern route — but with the

---

[25] Executive Office of the President, Energy Policy and Planning, *Decision and Report to Congress on the Alaska Natural Gas Transportation System* (Washington, D.C.: U.S. Government Printing Office, 1977), p. 107. The $10.3 billion figure was based on cost estimates filed with Canadian and U.S. regulatory bodies.

U.S. owners of the pipeline agreeing to pay for the connecting link between Whitehorse and Dawson when the decision to connect up the Mackenzie Delta gas was made. However, if cost overruns on the Canadian portion of the original pipeline exceeded 35 percent, the U.S. companies would pay less than the total cost of the connecting link, although not less than two-thirds. The additional cost of the Whitehorse-Dawson link was estimated to be less than that of taking a northern route from the beginning. Hence the United States would benefit from a decreased capital cost for the project, including the Dawson link, and from a certain protection against cost overruns on the Canadian portions of the Alaska Highway portion of the pipeline. Canada would benefit from having to pay only one-third, at most, of the cost of the connection to Dawson.

Another contentious area in the negotiations was a $200 million payment to the Yukon for the socio-economic costs associated with the building of the pipeline.[26] The United States did not want to go along with Canadian demands to pay such costs for fear of setting a precedent that would be applied in the United States. Finally it was agreed that the company building the Yukon portion of the pipeline would make an advance payment of $200 million against Yukon property taxes. Canada, in return, agreed to limit annual property taxes on the company to $30 million plus an adjustment for inflation. In this way Canada received the $200 million for socio-economic costs it was seeking, and the United States got assurances about the limits it could expect on Canadian property taxes, a matter of some uncertainty to U.S. planners of the pipeline.

Other concerns about the costs and benefits of the pipeline project were not so clearly defined by the agreement. The main unresolved question was the extent to which the goods and services required to build the pipeline, particularly the actual pipe and the pumping-station equipment, would be supplied by domestic industries. In the negotiations the United States wanted assurances that Canada would not force the companies building the Canadian section to accept high-cost bids to boost Canadian content. Canada, meanwhile, wanted protection from low bids by foreign suppliers with surplus productive capacity, which, it feared, could cut into the potential benefits construction of the pipeline would have for the Canadian economy. The agreement states that supplies of goods and services should be on generally competitive terms; but rather than specifying that contracts be limited to suppliers from one country or be open, it makes provision for governmental consultation to renegotiate contracts or reopen bids if necessary.

---

[26]The proposal for $200 million in compensation to the Yukon was originally made in the report of an inquiry on the Alaska Highway project, chaired by Kenneth Lysyk (Kenneth M. Lysyk, Edith E. Bohmer, and Willard L. Phelps, *Alaska Highway Pipeline Inquiry* [Ottawa: Supply and Services Canada, 1977], pp. 150-53).

In Canada there was considerable criticism of the pipeline agreement because of the lack of guarantees for Canadian content. Two developments subsequently eased these fears. First, the pipe that the National Energy Board has recommended for most of the Canadian portion of the project can be supplied entirely by Canadian pipe manufacturers.[27] Second, the Canadian government has set up an agency to supervise pipeline construction and the drawing up of any contracts with suppliers. Any uncertainty about Canadian content that remains mainly concerns financing of the pipeline; this, in turn, depends on energy legislation in the United States. Only when U.S. energy policy is settled will it be possible to determine the price structure for Alaskan natural gas and the likely rate of return on investment in the pipeline, and thus where it will be possible to obtain financing. If sufficient Canadian and U.S. equity financing cannot be found and foreign investors are brought in, the pressure to accept foreign contracts will increase.[28]

The negotiation of the Alaska Highway natural gas pipeline agreement is indicative of the improvement in relations between Canada and the United States and of the interest in cooperation in dealing with difficult energy problems. At the same time, this effort at cooperation is not without its risks. There are many uncertainties associated with this gigantic project, and if it were perceived to be not mutually advantageous to both countries, it could precipitate a rift in relations. There are certainly those who feel that their respective national interests would be better served by not being involved in a joint project. Some Americans would have preferred the LNG scheme because all the investment would have been to the benefit of the U.S. economy. Some Canadians feel that, if development of the Mackenzie Delta-Beaufort Sea area is not justified, the energy-investment resources of the country would be better devoted to projects of more direct benefit to Canada, such as additional tar sands

---

[27] The National Energy Board has selected a 56-inch-diameter, thin-walled, low-pressure pipe. The United States would have preferred a 48-inch-diameter, thick-walled, high-pressure pipe, of which Canadian pipe manufacturers would have been able to supply only 75 percent of requirements under the planned construction schedule. The U.S. preference was based mainly on the belief that the 48-inch pipe would result in lower gas transportation costs; the NEB preferred the 56-inch pipe because its performance in terms of safety is quite predictable compared to that of the 48-inch pipe, which would represent an innovation and would have to undergo extensive testing before it could be used.

[28] Even when the price picture becomes clear, Canadian and U.S. investors may be hesitant because the size of the project is disproportionately large in relation to the size of the companies involved. The combined assets of the gas transmission companies that will own the $10 billion pipeline are only $26 billion (*Business Week*, November 28, 1977). In addition, the U.S. government has made it clear that it will not subsidize or guarantee any part of the project, and it has agreed with the Canadian government that it will not allow the three large oil companies that own the bulk of the reserves at Prudhoe Bay (Exxon, Arco, and BP-Sohio) to take any equity interest in the project.

recovery plants, a polar gas pipeline, or a pipeline to convey Alberta gas to consumers in eastern Quebec and the Maritime provinces.

Canadian Gas Exports to the United States

It is estimated that the Alaska Highway natural gas pipeline will facilitate delivery of about 1.5 trillion cubic feet of natural gas per year when it comes on stream. Until then, the United States will continue to have a major need for natural gas in excess of its own production; and even after Alaskan gas is available, potential natural gas demand is expected to far exceed supply.[29] Canada has contracts to supply natural gas to the United States into the 1990s, but no new applications have been accepted by the National Energy Board since 1970. The gas surplus that has emerged in Canada's conventional producing areas in the past two years raises three possibilities for Canadian gas exports to the United States, each of which would improve Canadian gas producers' profitability and encourage more exploration:

• Canada could accelerate its sales to the United States under existing export contracts for the next five years or so to take advantage of excess productive capacity and to help ease supply problems in the United States until Alaskan gas becomes available.

• New contracts for additional exports could be drawn up. The probability of eventually tapping the Mackenzie Delta-Beaufort Sea gas adds to the feasibility of new contracts; but politically it seems unlikely, especially in view of the Canadian government's apparent support for extending Canada's natural-gas-pipeline system to new markets in eastern Quebec and the Maritime provinces.

• Canada could export gas in excess of existing contracts on condition that these supplies be made up when Alaskan gas started flowing. Such "time swaps" seem the most likely of the three to occur, despite the difficulty in arranging contracts that would reflect fairly the differences in the costs of gas delivered from two different sources at two different times.[30]

Any of these gas-export arrangements would make attractive the building of the southern portion of the Alaska Highway pipeline first. To have a section of the pipeline earning revenue at an early stage could have a beneficial effect on the financing for the entire project. One complication in initiating a new export arrangement,

---

[29] U.S. production of natural gas in 1976 was 19.1 trillion cubic feet; without Prudhoe Bay gas an optimistic projection is that domestic production would decline to 17.5 trillion cubic feet by 1985. It is estimated that potential natural gas demand in the United States is currently 25-30 trillion cubic feet per year (Executive Office of the President, *Decision and Report, op. cit.*, pp. 87-88).

[30] In March, 1978, Pan-Alberta Gas Limited of Calgary and Northwest Alaskan Pipeline Corporation of Salt Lake City signed two gas-swap contracts for one billion cubic feet per day, with deliveries expected to begin in late 1979 or in 1980.

however, is that the Alberta government has indicated that it is unwilling to increase its gas exports unless it receives "some tangible benefits for the people of Alberta," in the form of trade concessions with the United States, for its exports of certain agricultural and petrochemical products. Such concessions were discussed as part of a gas-swap package when U.S. Vice-President Mondale visited Ottawa and Alberta in January, 1978; but because such concessions will have to be negotiated on a multilateral basis under the GATT, any new export flows could be appreciably delayed if this commitment has to be met first.

Other Energy Questions

While the phasing out of Canadian oil exports and the decision to build the Alaskan gas pipeline have clearly been the most important Canada-U.S. energy concerns, they have by no means been the only ones in this period of worldwide energy readjustments. This section briefly reviews several other bilateral energy developments that have attracted attention in the past two years.

Strategic Oil Storage

Under their obligations to the International Energy Agency (IEA), Canada and the United States have agreed to maintain oil stockpiles as insurance against another oil embargo or production cutbacks by the major oil exporters.[31] The United States is already building up a strategic petroleum reserve of 500 million barrels, and President Carter's energy plan calls for expansion of this to one billion barrels. Canada has been relying on normal oil-industry inventories to meet its obligations to the IEA, and government officials feel Canada has a storage and pipeline network sufficient to continue meeting its obligations until 1985.

The capital costs of constructing facilities to store larger volumes of oil, as well as the carrying charges involved, make stockpiling very expensive.[32] One way to reduce the cost considerably is to store the oil in natural or man-made but unused underground areas rather than in steel tanks above ground. The United States will place the first 500 million barrels of its stockpile in salt caverns in the Gulf Coast region. For a certain portion of the second 500 million barrels, the U.S. government is interested in sites in other parts

---

[31] One aim of the International Energy Program, established in November, 1974, by the International Energy Agency, is "development of a common level of emergency self-sufficiency in oil supplies" (Organisation for Economic Co-operation and Development, *World Energy Outlook* [Paris, 1977], p. 2).

[32] The one-billion-barrel U.S. stockpile would cost an estimated $20 billion. There is concern in the U.S. Administration that the cost of the extra 500 million barrels will thwart President Carter's plan to balance the federal budget by 1981 (see *Business Week*, December 5, 1977).

of the country. Because there are few promising sites in the north-eastern United States, the U.S. government has expressed interest in Canadian proposals for use of possible storage sites in eastern Canada, particularly an abandoned iron ore mine in Newfoundland and salt domes in Nova Scotia, each of which could hold close to 100 million barrels. A joint Canada-U.S. study to examine the feasibility of such proposals recommended in a report in July, 1978, that the two governments begin negotiations on arrangements to develop the Canadian sites.

The storage of oil for strategic purposes may eventually have noteworthy bilateral implications in two respects. First, because the United States has indicated it would feel more comfortable about having part of its strategic stockpile in Canada if it were sharing the storage facility with the Canadian government, the scheme could result in a new form of joint Canada-U.S. initiative in the energy area. Second, because the storage of U.S. oil supplies in Canada could provide the guarantee that Canada would need to permit time swaps of oil, the scheme could facilitate greater flows of Canadian oil to the Northern Tier states for a limited period. Time swaps have been discussed bilaterally, but because the companies that would be involved have shown so much apprehension about pricing over time (similar to the situation with time swaps of gas, mentioned above), they seem a long way from materializing.

Liquified-Natural-Gas Imports

The Alaska Highway natural gas pipeline is not the only joint gas-transportation proposal that has been under consideration in the past two years. A group of Canadian and U.S. companies have applied to build a system to deliver Algerian natural gas to markets in the northeastern United States through a pipeline originating in Canada. The project, headed by Tenneco Inc. of Houston, Texas, would consist of transporting the gas from Algeria as liquified natural gas in specially built tankers to a terminal near Saint John, New Brunswick, where it would be regasified and shipped by a new, 500-mile pipeline to supply Tenneco's pipeline network in New York and Pennsylvania. The National Energy Board announced condi-tional approval of the Canadian portion of the project on December 17, 1977, and a decision by the U.S. Department of Energy was pending at the time this was written.

As in the case of the Alaska Highway pipeline, Canada's main interest, in the initial project at least, is in the construction benefits, since most of the gas will be destined for U.S. markets and the facil-ity will employ relatively few people once in operation.[33] Eventually,

---

[33] One of the conditions set by the National Energy Board in granting approval for building the Canadian portion of the project was that up to 5 percent of the total gas imported from Algeria be available for possible sale in Canada.

however, the terminal could be used for landing LNG from Canada's Arctic islands. It is anticipated in Canada that at some point it may be feasible to use Arctic island gas to supply Canada's eastern market or for export to the eastern United States.

Emergency Supplies of Energy

The winter of 1976/77 was one of the coldest on record in the United States, resulting in fuel shortages over large areas of the country. Canada responded quickly to the U.S. emergency by providing supplies of oil and natural gas that were in addition to normal exports. The National Energy Board permitted emergency exports of 800 thousand barrels of crude oil, 2.5 million barrels of oil products, and 36.6 billion cubic feet of natural gas, as well as pre-delivery of 200 thousand barrels of light crude.[34] In addition, when severe weather conditions caused a serious breakdown in two Michigan power utilities for a brief period, Ontario Hydro was able to provide assistance by instituting a province-wide voltage reduction.[35]

Canada's willingness to help the United States overcome its energy emergency symbolizes the underlying strength of the relationship between the two countries.

Trade in Coal

In contrast to the situation with oil and gas, the United States is a net exporter of coal, and Canada is a major market. In 1977 Canada imported 16.5 million tons of U.S. coal; about half was thermal coal, mostly for Ontario Hydro, and the rest was metallurgical coal to meet the coking requirements of Canada's steel industry. Overall, Canada has been a small net importer of coal, since producers in the western provinces make sizable exports. (Canada exported 13.3 million tons in 1977, of which 11.4 million tons went to Japan.)

Coal-fired plants account for about 25 percent of Ontario Hydro's energy production, and the U.S. Appalachian region has been supplying most of the coal. Despite a solid commitment to nuclear power, Ontario Hydro expects its coal requirements to continue to grow well into the 1980s. To diversify its sources of supply somewhat, Ontario Hydro has indicated it would like to have Western Canada provide about 4 million of an estimated 7 million tons of additional requirements by the early 1980s.[36] A new terminal at

---

[34] National Energy Board internal communication.

[35] For a history of electricity interconnections see Mark Perlgut, *Electricity Across the Border: The U.S.-Canadian Experience* (Montreal and Washington: Canadian-American Committee, 1978).

[36] See The Bank of Nova Scotia, "Opportunities and Challenges for Western Canada's Coal Industry," *Monthly Review*, January, 1976.

Thunder Bay to transfer coal from rail to ship is scheduled to open in 1978. It will increase the capacity for moving coal into Ontario from a current maximum of 1.5 million tons a year to 6 million tons. In addition, Canadian steel producers have been testing Western Canadian coal, and it seems likely that they too will be using it to some appreciable extent by the 1980s.

Security of supply has been cited as one reason for moving to more expensive Western Canadian coal.[37] However, this concern is undoubtedly more a reaction to the general perception of an energy-short world than to any specific threat by U.S. suppliers or the U.S. government. The United States has enormous reserves of coal, and Canada has always purchased its coal at prevailing U.S. prices. Embargoes on exports to Canada have never been imposed. Canada's demands on the U.S. coal market, moreover, are quite small, which is not the case for U.S. demands on the Canadian oil and gas markets.[38] On the other hand, one of the main planks of the U.S. energy policy introduced by President Carter is an increased emphasis on coal. The Administration's program includes a coal-conservation plan that proposes to use tax and regulatory measures to encourage industries and utilities to shift from oil and natural gas to coal. While at no point has this plan suggested changing export policy, Canadian purchasers of U.S. coal would probably, at the very least, experience some price effects. To limit exports would be inconsistent with an aim of the IEA, which the United States has endorsed, to expand world use of thermal coal to reduce dependence on oil.[39]

Trade in Uranium

Canada and the United States are both major world suppliers of uranium, but trade between the two countries has been negligible in recent years. In 1966 the United States passed legislation that effectively banned all imports of uranium, a move that created major difficulties for Canada's uranium industry, which had been supplying a quarter of U.S. needs. A program to relax the import controls was begun in 1977, and all restrictions will be removed by 1984. This could pave the way for substantial Canadian exports to the United States: the ability of U.S. uranium reserves to meet U.S. domestic requirements and export commitments has been a subject of some concern recently, especially in view of the policy announced by President Carter in April, 1977, to defer indefinitely the reprocessing

[37] See address by Malcolm Rowan, Deputy Minister of the Ontario Ministry of Energy, to the 28th Canadian Conference on Coal, Ottawa, September 26-28, 1976. Mr. Rowan cites factors that lead him to the conclusion that Western Canadian coal "is up to 50 percent more expensive than coal from the U.S."

[38] For more detail on the prospects for trade in coal between the two countries, see Richard L. Gordon, *Coal and Canada-U.S. Energy Relations* (Montreal and Washington: Canadian-American Committee, 1976).

[39] OECD, *op. cit.*

and recycling of spent fuel and the development of the more fuel-efficient fast-breeder reactor.[40] On November 15, 1977, Canada and the United States concluded an interim agreement permitting Canadian uranium to be used in U.S. nuclear reactors.

As a result of this agreement Canada was able to clear up problems with its exports of uranium to Japan. In 1974 the Canadian government implemented new conditions governing uranium exports, one of which was that countries purchasing uranium agree to safeguards against the use of nuclear materials and technology for weapons, a reaction to the detonation by India of a nuclear device built with plutonium from a Canadian-built reactor. When compliance with the safeguard demands had not been reached by the beginning of 1977, Canada placed an embargo on exports to Japan, the European Economic Community, and Switzerland. Much of the Canadian uranium destined for foreign markets goes first to the United States for enrichment. One of the major difficulties in reaching an agreement on safeguards with Japan was that Japan did not want to have to meet the conditions of both Canada and the United States on imports of uranium originating in Canada and being enriched in the United States. The Canada-U.S. agreement was designed so that Japan would have the option of complying with its obligations to Canada via the United States, which in turn would seek Canadian approval for control rights held by both Canada and the United States. With the resolution of this difficulty it was possible to conclude a Canada-Japan agreement in January, 1978, to permit renewed Canadian exports of uranium to Japan. An interim agreement on safeguards to allow Canada to export uranium to the EEC was also worked out in January, 1978.

Energy: A Summary

Canada-U.S. energy relations have shown a marked turn for the better in the past two years:

• U.S. concern over Canada's decision to phase out oil exports has diminished as Canadians have demonstrated a willingness to assist Northern Tier refineries in the short run by permitting oil exchanges and in the long run by entertaining proposals for transportation systems across Canadian territory to supply that area.

• An agreement, which may be of considerable benefit to both countries, has been negotiated so that a pipeline can be built to transport natural gas from Alaska to the Lower 48 states across Canada. When, seven years earlier, the decision was taken to move

---

[40] For more detail on the prospects for trade in uranium between the two countries, see Hugh C. McIntyre, *Uranium, Nuclear Power, and Canada-U.S. Energy Relations* (Montreal and Washington: Canadian-American Committee, 1978).

Alaskan oil to southern markets, a system was chosen that did not involve crossing Canada.[41]

• Discussions on a wide variety of bilateral energy issues have been conducted in a friendly and cooperative mood.

In general, these developments reflect a recognition that the two countries face quite similar energy problems. Americans now realize that Canada is not a land of virtually limitless energy resources, and Canadians themselves no longer look upon their situation as being particularly favorable. Conservation has become a central theme in the energy policies of both countries.

However, despite cooperation with the United States on so many energy questions, Canada has continued to resist any movement toward a continental sharing of energy resources. It is still acutely conscious of the enormous appetite of the U.S. market compared to its own and continues to protect its domestic energy resources. Because the United States has been willing to accept Canada's interpretation of its own resource potential, moreover, pressure for a continental approach seems less in evidence. In the instances where Canada has an abundance of an energy resource, the situation is in most cases recognized by both sides to be only a temporary one.

The solutions to the energy problems of both Canada and the United States lie in a long-range approach involving conservation, the development of renewable energy sources, and development of technology to unlock the huge, untapped supplies of fossil fuels in the oil shales and oil sands. The cooperation demonstrated in the past two years provides hope that the two countries will be able to work together in these important areas.

Some Non-Energy-Resource Concerns

The remainder of this chapter examines a number of other, mostly non-related, non-energy, bilateral resource questions, a review of which is needed to complete an overall picture of Canada-U.S. relations in the resource field. In several cases long-standing bilateral frictions are reviewed; other cases are unique to the past two years. The areas covered include

• the negotiations going on to determine the boundary between Canada and the United States in the extended territorial sea;

• the debate, under the auspices of the Law of the Sea Conference, on the effects of deep-seabed mining on the world nickel industry;

---

[41] Of course, there are also other factors that were relevant to the Trans-Alaska Pipeline System decision to move North Slope oil by tanker from Valdez. Oil is more easily shipped by tanker than is gas, which must first be converted to LNG. Moreover, the United States wanted access to Alaskan oil as early as possible and feared that it would take too long for a project across Canada to get clearance from regulatory agencies.

- the extraterritorial implications of the U.S. investigation of a uranium producers' cartel;
- the actions of some provincial governments in Canada to take over certain resource industries; and
- the progress taking place in resolving cross-border environmental concerns.

Setting Maritime Boundaries

Even though negotiations are continuing on other matters, a consensus has been reached at the Third United Nations Law of the Sea Conference on the concept of a 200-mile economic zone in which coastal states would have sovereignty over living and non-living resources and jurisdiction over the prevention and control of marine pollution.[42] Sensing that the conclusion of the Law of the Sea Conference was still a long way off, Canada (on January 1, 1977) and the United States (on March 1, 1977) extended their fisheries zones to 200 miles, claiming that this seemed the only way to halt the rapid depletion of fish stocks resulting from extensive operations by fishermen of many nations and to arrest the decline of their own fishing industries. A number of other countries have also taken this step.

The establishment of a 200-mile limit necessitates a country's dealing with two points: the degree of access foreign countries will have to fisheries within the 200-mile limit and the extensions of existing boundaries between countries. Canada and the United States have handled the first point by each negotiating with the major fishing nations agreements setting the terms under which these countries would be permitted to fish within its 200-mile limit. As far as bilateral fishing rights are concerned, Canada and the United States established an interim agreement for 1977 which allowed fishermen to fish without licenses in each other's waters and at the same level as in 1976. Eventually, reciprocal fishing rights will be incorporated into a formal boundary treaty. When the formal treaty had not been negotiated by the end of 1977 (as explained below), an interim fishing agreement modeled on the 1977 agreement was worked out to cover 1978. The 1978 agreement, however, contained several new provisions; and when differences involving these could not be resolved, Canada, on June 2, 1978, closed its waters to U.S. fishermen. The United States reacted immediately by closing its waters to Canadians.[43] Both governments have indicated regret that

---

[42]The Third United Nations Law of the Sea Conference began in Caracas, Venezuela, in the summer of 1974. As of mid-1978, seven formal negotiating sessions had been held without a comprehensive Law of the Sea convention emerging.

[43]The 1978 interim agreement contained stronger provisions for consultation on the management of common fish stocks, as well as provisions permitting Canadian salmon fishermen more favorable access to U.S. west coast waters. These changes reflected the feeling by Canada that certain regulatory actions by the United States

these difficulties with the interim agreement have occurred and have stated their continued dedication to working out a formal boundary treaty.

Several principles can be applied to the drawing of the boundary extensions to the 200-mile limit, and Canada and the United States have tended to take different positions.[44] For example, in the Gulf of Maine between New England and the Maritime provinces — an area with extremely fertile fishing grounds and possibly rich hydrocarbon deposits — the United States feels the line should follow the Northeast Channel, thus putting all of Georges Bank in the United States. Canada favors a line that runs equidistant between the two countries and thereby puts part of Georges Bank in Canada. The other three boundaries that must be decided upon are at the entrance of the Strait of Juan de Fuca between British Columbia and the state of Washington, the Dixon Entrance between British Columbia and Alaska, and in the Beaufort Sea between Alaska and the Yukon.

On August 1, 1977, both countries appointed special negotiators to conduct discussions aimed at reaching a settlement of the maritime boundary and related resource issues.[45] The approach of the negotiators has been to place priority on obtaining agreement on the maritime-resource issues in the hope of making settlement of the actual boundaries easier. In their reports the negotiators have recommended the establishment of a joint Canada-U.S. fisheries commission for the cooperative management of fish stocks of common concern.[46] Fish stocks would be divided into three management categories: clearly transboundary stocks would be managed by the fisheries commission itself; stocks of primary interest to one country would be managed through the commission, mainly on the basis of the proposals of the country with primary interest; and stocks

---

in 1977 had hurt the catch of Canadian fishermen. In exchange for these adjustments in the interim agreement, the United States wanted Canada to close its west coast Swiftsure Bank fishery as a conservation measure during the period April 15 to June 15, when many of the salmon there are of U.S. origin. When Canada did not close the Swiftsure Bank because its conservation experts felt it was unnecessary, the United States withdrew the new salmon privileges for Canadian fishermen on the U.S. west coast. On the east coast, Canada was upset by what it considered to be excessive allowable U.S. catch levels for haddock and cod and unrestricted fishing of pollock and scallops in zones shared by the two countries. Canada had hoped these problems would be overcome through the consultative provision in the 1978 interim agreement. It was because of the problems on both coasts that Canada closed its waters to U.S. fishermen.

[44] For a discussion of marine boundaries in general and of the Canada-U.S. question in particular, see R. M. Logan, *Canada, the United States, and the Third Law of the Sea Conference* (Montreal and Washington: Canadian-American Committee, 1974), pp. 53-68.

[45] The special negotiators appointed were Marcel Cadieux for Canada and Lloyd Cutler for the United States.

[46] Department of External Affairs, "Communiqué," October 21, 1977, and March 28, 1978.

clearly occurring off the coast of only one country would be managed by that country in consultation with the commission. With respect to hydrocarbon resources in boundary areas, the negotiators propose using "shared access zones" in which each country would be responsible for oil and gas licensing and development in its portion of the zone and entitled to one-half the production from the entire zone.

Originally the negotiators were to have presented their proposal for a comprehensive settlement to the boundary and resource issues by December 1, 1977, but as of July, 1978, there were still problems to be solved. Nevertheless, the negotiators have continued to indicate they believe an acceptable comprehensive settlement can be reached. If it cannot, both sides have agreed to consider third-party assistance.

Deep-Seabed Mining

The issue that, more than any other, has held up agreement on a new comprehensive Law of the Sea convention is that of mining in the seabed beyond the 200-mile limit. At stake is the harvesting of nodules containing nickel, cobalt, manganese, and copper known to lie on the ocean floor. On one point in the negotiations over deep-seabed mining — how seabed nickel production should be incorporated into the existing nickel market — the Canadian and U.S. positions have been in conflict.

The origins of this conflict go back to the second formal working session of the Law of the Sea Conference in Geneva in 1975, where a difference of views was established between the United States and other developed countries, who wanted private mining interests to have access to seabed minerals, and many of the developing countries, who felt access should be limited to governments or state-owned corporations and to an international seabed authority.[47] The Single Negotiating Text which emerged from the Geneva meeting embraced the position of the developing countries. The dispute carried over to the next session in New York in the spring of 1976. At the last moment the U.S. delegation made a compromise proposal. In return for assurances of a place for private companies in deep-seabed mining, the private companies would hand over some of their fully explored mine sites, as well as the technology they had developed, to help the international authority get started in mining. One of the reasons for opposition to private corporations' being involved had been the fear that they would be able to gear up their operations much more quickly than an international authority, so that the benefits of seabed mining would accrue to the developed countries long before they accrued to the developing countries. To further enhance

---

[47]The developing countries were proposing that revenue from the operation of the international authority be shared as one way of allocating the benefits of the sea as "the common heritage of mankind."

the prospects of getting an early return from the operations of the international authority, the U.S. proposal called for a formula that would permit the seabed-mining segment of the nickel industry to supply the annual increase in world demand — which, on the basis of postwar trends, would be assumed to be 6 percent. When the Revised Single Negotiating Text came out only a few days after the U.S. proposal was made known, it incorporated the proposal.

The Canadian delegation was upset by the U.S. proposal for several reasons. First, the Canadians had been given no prior indication of what the U.S. delegation was planning. Apparently, some countries did know in advance because some of the developing nations that are large, land-based copper producers had met with the U.S. delegates to seek assurances that copper, which is tied to nickel in the seabed nodules, would not be used as the basis for a production formula. Because Canada has never expressed protectionist sentiments about copper, it was not involved in these discussions.[48] Second, the proposal was made at such a late stage in the session that there was no opportunity to discuss it in the relevant committee prior to the assembly of the Revised Single Negotiating Text. Third, and most important, Canada is the world's largest producer of nickel, and the proposal represented a direct threat to its land-based nickel industry. Denying access to growth in demand could wipe out all incentive for new investment in the Canadian industry. Moreover, if long-term growth in nickel demand turns out to be less than 6 percent, as the Canadian government believes it will, and if seabed production were at 6 percent, the Canadian industry would face a shrinking market.

The Canadian government has always favored the orderly development of seabed mining; a number of Canadian mining companies are participants in seabed-mining consortiums. Canada proposed that seabed-mining interests be given full rights to growth in the market for the first five years after the commencement of commercial production and that subsequent seabed production be limited to supplying up to 50 percent of the growth in demand. There has been a move toward a formula somewhat in this style in the Law of the Sea committee as well; in the Informal Composite Negotiating Text, which emerged from the sixth session in July, 1977, the production formula called for seabed-mining interests to have rights to 60 percent of the cumulative increase in world demand after 1980 and, to help launch seabed mining, to have exclusive rights to incremental world demand for the first seven years after 1980. In the seventh session in May, 1978, the formula was altered to permit the seabed sector to absorb 100 percent of the increase in demand for five years and 60 percent thereafter, and the means by which the

---

[48]This explanation is given by columnist Geoffrey Stevens (*Globe and Mail* [Toronto], May 13, 1976).

growth in demand would be calculated was altered so that the growth would work out to be less than 6 percent annually. There seems to be considerable optimism that this formula will be acceptable to Canada, the United States, and the world's developing countries.

Agreement on conventions for administering the deep seabed have been held up by more than just the future-market-shares issue, but this is the issue mainly relevant to Canada-U.S. relations.[49] Support in the United States for deep-seabed mining exists because it offers an opportunity to greatly reduce U.S. dependence on imports (currently, U.S. production accounts for only about 6 percent of U.S. nickel requirements) and because U.S. mining corporations are eager to develop this new source of raw materials. The U.S. proposal was made in the hope that it would permit U.S. objectives to be achieved and at the same time provide for the operation of the international authority that many other countries want. U.S. officials have indicated that their proposal was not intended to harm the Canadian industry or to represent a deterioration in bilateral relations.[50]

Uranium-Cartel Investigation

It is a common characteristic of the present world economic system that the boundaries of business activity do not correspond to national boundaries. Frequently the laws a company may be forced to abide by in one country are in conflict with those of another country in which it operates, possibly to the economic detriment of one country or the other. Such cross-boundary differences have been a continuing feature of Canada-U.S. relations. Several years ago, for example, a U.S. embargo on trade with Cuba — a country with which Canada had no embargo — put Canadian subsidiaries of U.S. companies in the difficult position of choosing between foregoing the Cuban market or risking violation of the U.S. Trading with the Enemy Act.

Probably the most visible example of the cross-border application of law in the past two years has been the investigation in the United States of an international uranium producers' marketing association, of which Canada was a member. In response to a depressed

---

[49] Other issues include the structure of the proposed international seabed authority, which the developed countries claim discriminates against countries with the technology and the desire to mine the seabed (these countries would have only 4 of 36 executive-council seats), and the provision that would force private mining companies to turn their operations over to the international authority if, following a compulsory review after twenty years of seabed mining, agreement could not be reached within five years to extend or amend the rules and procedures for private mining companies.

[50] Canadian External Affairs Minister Allan MacEachen received such assurances from U.S. Secretary of State Henry Kissinger shortly after the issue arose (*Globe and Mail* [Toronto], May 11, 1976).

world uranium market, representatives of the governments of Canada, France, and Australia and of producers from Canada, France, Australia, South Africa, and Britain met in 1972 to establish a Uranium Marketing Research Organization, purportedly to be a forum for discussing the industry's problems. In 1976, as part of an investigation of anti-trust violations, the U.S. Justice Department launched a federal grand jury investigation of this organization to try to assess whether it had acted as a cartel to cause significant increases in world uranium prices. A second investigation was started in November, 1976, by the U.S. House of Representatives Subcommittee on Oversight and Investigation. A third investigation was begun in February, 1977, when Westinghouse Electric Corporation took action against twenty-nine companies it alleged had participated in, or collaborated with, members of the cartel. Westinghouse had been sued by several U.S. electric utilities that had bought Westinghouse reactors for which Westinghouse was unable to meet its commitments to supply uranium fuel because of a sharp increase in world uranium prices.

The last two investigations revealed that, in the 1972-75 period, Canada participated in a uranium cartel that set minimum and maximum prices for uranium and decided on market shares. The Canadian government has defended its participation in the marketing group on the grounds that it was necessary to protect its uranium industry and the communities dependent upon it. Canada's uranium industry had been developed in the 1950s largely to supply the U.S. market. In 1966 the United States put an embargo on imports of uranium, thus barring Canadian producers from 70 percent of the non-Communist world market of the time. The Canadian government tried to assist producers by establishing a stockpiling scheme and, in 1970, by initiating discussions with customers for Canadian uranium to alleviate the marketing problems. When these efforts failed to provide sufficient relief, the government authorized marketing arrangements with other international producers. In the face of the findings by the investigations in the United States, Canada has claimed that the cartel could not have affected the U.S. market because, except for two brief periods, prices of U.S. domestic producers were higher than those set by the cartel and because the U.S. market was largely closed to foreign uranium producers by the embargo anyway.[51]

The motivation for the U.S. investigations can be linked to a sensitivity about energy prices following the sharp jump in oil prices in 1973 and about the operations of cartels in view of the role of OPEC in that oil-price hike. Between 1972 and 1975 the price of

---

[51] Under the terms of the 1966 embargo, U.S. utilities were permitted to buy foreign uranium for stockpiling or for future delivery in anticipation of removal of the embargo.

uranium rose from $6 to over $20 a pound. Moreover, the United States decided in 1974 to start lifting its import embargo on uranium in 1977, so it was beginning to be more conscious of the condition of world markets.

Canadian government officials, as well as the officials of other countries involved in the cartel, have been disturbed by the U.S. investigations on several counts. First, Canada was upset that the actions of Canadian uranium producers, which were required by Canadian law and taken in accordance with Canadian policy, should be called into question by foreign courts. In late 1976 the Canadian government passed Uranium Information Security Regulations to prevent the release of information relating to uranium-marketing arrangements. Failure to take such action would have placed the government in the untenable position of allowing evidence to be provided to a foreign court for use in the possible prosecution of Canadian nationals for acts that were in accordance with Canadian law and policy. Second, Canada was upset that the House of Representatives subcommittee decided to make public documents, including those of the Canadian government, that had been obtained from Gulf Oil Corporation and that had originated with Gulf's Canadian uranium-mining subsidiary, Gulf Minerals Canada Limited. Canada protested that the documents contained information about its relations with third countries that should not be made public and that in Canada this information was confidential under the Official Secrets Act.[52] Representative John Moss, chairman of the subcommittee, contended that any consideration of courteous relations between the Canadian and the U.S. governments on this issue was overriden by the Canadian government's commercial interest in the proceedings through its ownership of Eldorado Nuclear Limited, a crown corporation involved in uranium mining.[53] Finally, aside from the embarrassment that the revelations about secret involvement in cartel activities have caused, Canada felt it had a legitimate reason to be concerned about the uranium investigations because of their extraterritorial implications. Subsidiaries of U.S. companies operating in Canada would be inclined to lean toward U.S. law as a result of these proceedings.

Although not all the information needed to piece together the full uranium-cartel story has been released, ultimately the investigation is probably at least as significant, from a bilateral perspective, as the actual operations of the cartel. There is considerable doubt that the cartel has had any major effect on the long-run price of uranium, although it probably did affect the pace of the price

---

[52] Gulf Minerals claims that the documents obtained by the House of Representatives subcommittee were sent to the United States before the Uranium Information Security Regulations were passed in late 1976.

[53] *Gazette* (Montreal), June 10, 1977.

increases in the 1972-75 period.[54] The investigation, on the other hand, is an example of the extraterritorial application of U.S. law, a recurring theme in Canada-U.S. relations.[55] From the investigation, however, some hope for better handling of such issues in the future has been generated. Government officials, led by Canadian Justice Minister Ron Basford and U.S. Attorney General Griffin Bell, agreed in June, 1977, to set up an "early warning system" to be used to defuse irritants when the anti-trust laws of one country affect the citizens or companies of the other.

Takeovers in Resource Industries

In the past three years the possibility of government takeover has emerged as a major new source of uncertainty for private investment in natural-resource industries in Canada. The threat has arisen as a direct result of the desire of provincial governments (who have the ownership rights to resources within their boundaries) to increase the returns from the exploitation of their resources. In November, 1975, the government of Saskatchewan announced that it would take over at least half of the potash industry in that province. Canada produces about 25 percent of the world's potash, and all Canadian mines now in operation are located in Saskatchewan. By early 1978 the Potash Corporation of Saskatchewan, the crown corporation set up to operate the province's potash interests, had purchased four of the ten mines in the province and 60 percent ownership of a fifth.[56] In October, 1977, the government of Quebec announced that it would take over controlling interest in Asbestos Corporation Limited, the third-largest asbestos producer in Canada.[57] Canada accounts for about one-third of world asbestos production, 80 percent of which comes from Quebec. In both cases, expropriation was indicated as a possibility if appropriate purchase prices could not be worked out. The significance of these take-

---

[54]For a more complete assessment of the price effects of the uranium cartel, see D. J. Lecraw, "The Uranium Cartel: An Interim Report," *The Business Quarterly*, Winter, 1977.

[55]One explanation for the extraterritorial application of U.S. law generally is simply that "the United States is keener than other countries on the legal regulation of business activities" (*The Economist*, August 20, 1977, p. 78).

[56]In August, 1976, Saskatchewan purchased the mine of Duval Corporation of Canada, a subsidiary of Pennzoil United Inc. of Houston; in March, 1977, it bought the mine of Sylvite of Canada, a division of Hudson Bay Mining and Smelting Co., Limited of Toronto; in July, 1977, it acquired the property of Alwinsal Potash of Canada Limited, which had been jointly owned by French and West German mining interests; and in January, 1978, it bought the mine of Amax Potash Ltd. of Greenwich, Connecticut. Early in 1978 it also acquired 60 percent of the property of APM Operators Ltd. by purchasing the shares of United States Borax and Chemical Corporation of Los Angeles and of Swift Canadian Co. Limited of Toronto.

[57]According to Bernard Landry, the Quebec Minister of State for Economic Development, the Asbestos Corporation takeover is the only one the Quebec government is contemplating (*Globe and Mail* [Toronto], November 12, 1977).

overs for Canada-U.S. relations is that U.S. companies have invested heavily in Canadian resource industries and are involved, along with other foreign companies, in the takeovers in the potash and asbestos industries.

The Saskatchewan government's action was motivated by concern that too much of the return from production of a non-renewable resource was flowing to corporate mining interests and not enough to the province and its residents. The government first attempted to increase its share of the return from potash by increasing its taxes on the industry, but this served only to provoke confrontations on a fairly broad front between the industry and the government, including litigation. The tax increases were unsuccessful, partly because a failure of the federal and the provincial governments to reach an accord on resource-industry taxation resulted in an extremely heavy tax burden on resource industries and partly because relations between the government and the industry had been very strained to begin with.[58] The government subsequently chose the takeover route because it felt this was the only way to maximize the revenue to the province on a long-term basis.

In the case of asbestos, the Quebec government believes that, by taking over Asbestos Corporation Limited, it will be able to increase the further processing of asbestos within the province and thereby provide much-needed employment opportunities. At present only about 3 percent of Quebec's production is converted into finished products in the province; the government seeks to increase this to 10 to 20 percent.

Several aspects of the takeovers in potash and asbestos are pertinent to Canada-U.S. relations. Foreign ownership of Canadian resource industries does not appear to have been an important factor in the takeover decision. In the case of potash, the Canadian government has indicated to the U.S. government that it is aware of the possibility of discrimination but does not believe the Saskatchewan government has been guilty of unequal treatment against the nationals of various states.[59] With respect to compensation, the federal government has assured the U.S. government that it believes the provisions contained in the Saskatchewan legislation meet the requirements of international law.[60] Certainly the negotiations for the purchases of the mines seem to have gone smoothly, and the companies involved appear satisfied with the prices agreed upon. There has been some concern in the United States that the price or supply of Canadian potash to the U.S. market might be adversely affected

---

[58] For background to the events leading to the takeovers in the Saskatchewan potash industry, see Richard Shaffner, *HRI Observations*, No. 12, *New Risks in Resource Development: The Potash Case* (Montreal: C. D. Howe Research Institute, 1976).

[59] A note from the Canadian Department of External Affairs to the U.S. Embassy, March 23, 1976.

[60] *Ibid.*

by government ownership of the industry. So far there does not seem to be any evidence that this has occurred.

These takeovers have created a general uncertainty about private investment in resource industries in Canada; in the longer term, this may well be to the particular detriment of Saskatchewan and Quebec.[61]

Environmental Questions

The combination of a long border and a growing consciousness of the health of the natural environment in both Canada and the United States has been making bilateral environmental questions increasingly prominent. Consideration of environmental issues is included in this chapter because air and water, on which pollution concerns usually focus, are important natural resources and because pollution is frequently associated with the use of other resources, particularly energy. For example, there has been much concern on both the east and the west coasts about the danger of oil spills at prospective tanker terminals, and thermal power plants are one of the main causes of concern over air pollution.

The mechanism for dealing with Canada-U.S.-boundary environmental problems is well established. The two governments have developed effective methods for advance notification and consultation on potential and actual issues. In addition, the International Joint Commission, created by the Boundary Waters Treaty of 1909, can be requested by either government or by both governments to investigate and report on questions of water or air pollution. The IJC's recommendations are not binding; however, because they are based on impartial studies, almost without exception they have formed the basis for resolutions to problems.

There are currently about a dozen environmental issues attracting the attention of the two governments. Space does not permit a thorough review of these here, but it is worthwhile to indicate some of the most significant ones.

Water Quality

In most cases the area affected by a particular environmental concern is small. The main exception is the quality of water in the Great Lakes, which has by far the largest scope of any bilateral

---

[61] For example, in October, 1977, the Potash Company of America announced it had selected New Brunswick as the site for a $106 million potash development. The environment for private investment in Saskatchewan, where PCA had been operating a potash mine since 1965, was cited as the reason for the decision to expand in New Brunswick rather than in Saskatchewan. (*Globe and Mail* [Toronto], October 25, 1977.) In March, 1978, a second Saskatchewan potash producer, International Minerals and Chemical Corp. (Canada) Ltd., signed a potash-development agreement with New Brunswick.

environmental issue. In an all-out effort to deal with the problems of this large and heavily populated basin, the Canada-U.S. Great Lakes Water Quality Agreement was signed in 1972 to set common water-quality standards for effluents from municipal, industrial, and radioactive sources. According to the 1976 Annual Report of the IJC's Great Lakes Water Quality Board — which was established under the Agreement — between 1973 and 1976 the portion of the sewered population served by adequate treatment had increased from 84 to 99 percent on the Canadian side and from 35 to 62 percent on the U.S. side.[62] At the same time the Board indicated forty-seven areas where water-quality objectives were not being met and noted that progress in meeting industrial-effluent objectives was being hampered by the fact that the requirements were being contested by some companies. The efforts that have been marshalled under the Great Lakes Water Quality Board are beginning to result in improvements in water quality in zones close to shore and in an apparent halt to further deterioration of the main bodies of the Lakes. In May, 1978, Canadian and U.S. negotiators reached accord on a revised Great Lakes Water Quality Agreement to succeed the 1972 Agreement.

Among the most contentious of recent water-quality issues has been the Garrison Diversion Unit, which would divert water from the Missouri River system to irrigate about 250,000 acres of central and eastern North Dakota. As originally planned, most of the waste waters from the irrigated areas would drain into Manitoba through the Hudson Bay drainage basin. Canadians have opposed the Garrison project on the grounds that the leaching of the irrigated soils could degrade the quality of waters flowing into Canada, that the increase in flow could increase flooding, and that connecting the Missouri and the Hudson Bay drainage basins could result in the introduction of foreign fish, fish diseases, and fish parasites into Manitoba waters, where they would have a detrimental effect on the existing aquatic system and on commercial and recreational fishing. In February, 1974, and on several subsequent occasions, the government of the United States has given assurances that it will comply with its obligations under Article IV of the Boundary Waters Treaty and will not pollute water crossing the boundary.[63] In 1975 the IJC was asked to examine the transboundary implications of the Garrison Diversion Unit. In its report, presented to the two governments in 1977, it concluded that the project would result in adverse impacts on the water quality and biological resources of Manitoba,

---

[62] Great Lakes Water Quality Board, *Great Lakes Water Quality*, Fifth Annual Report to the International Joint Commission (Windsor, Ontario, 1977), p. 32.

[63] Article IV of the 1909 Boundary Waters Treaty reads in part as follows: "It is further agreed that the waters herein defined as boundary waters and waters flowing across the boundary shall not be polluted on either side to the injury of health or property on the other."

and it recommended that the portion of the project affecting waters flowing into Canada not be built until these problems were resolved.[64] In February, 1978, the U.S. Department of the Interior released a draft revised plan for the Garrison Diversion project, on which it has requested, and received, comments from the Canadian government. After more than ten years and an investment of $115 million, or 20 percent of its estimated total cost, the fate of the Garrison project remains uncertain.

Air Quality

For the most part, the air-quality issues that have been attracting attention are quite localized. Typical of these is the case of the Poplar River coal-fired power station in Saskatchewan, only four miles from the Montana border. Montana residents have been concerned that emissions from the plant will adversely affect the air quality in that region of the state adjacent to Saskatchewan, so that, among other things, new industries will be discouraged from locating there because it will be more difficult to meet U.S. environmental standards. At the request of the U.S. government, the IJC asked the International Air Pollution Advisory Board to review this matter. The Saskatchewan Power Corporation, the publicly owned utility constructing the plant, has agreed to install particulate removal equipment designed to achieve a 99 percent level of effectiveness. However, there is still concern in the United States about sulfur dioxide emissions because SPC will not be installing sulfur dioxide "scrubbers," which are not required to meet Canadian standards and which Canadian officials claim are not needed for Canada to meet its transboundary environmental obligations. There is also concern in the United States about the possible doubling of the size of the power plant by SPC.

In a quite similar case the United States has expressed concern about the possible threat to the fragile ecology of a wilderness area of northern Minnesota from the emissions of a projected coal-fired generating station at Atikokan, Ontario, about forty miles from the border.

A broader air-quality question gaining attention in the Canada-U.S. context is long-range air pollution — that is, the impact of pollutants that have been transported hundreds of miles from their origins. This problem has been under study in Northern Europe for some time and will be of greater relevance to North America if, as seems likely, coal becomes the source of a larger share of North American energy requirements.

---

[64] International Joint Commission, *Transboundary Implications of the Garrison Diversion Unit* (1977), pp. 121-23.

Coastal Pollution

The danger of oil spills from tankers approaching terminals has been a major bilateral concern on the east and west coasts and in the Arctic. The main controversy on the east coast involves the proposal to build an oil refinery at Eastport, Maine, which would mean that tankers carrying foreign crude would pass through waters adjacent to the Canadian coast. In December, 1976, the Canadian Department of Fisheries and the Environment released a report on the environmental risks associated with twenty-two possible oil-terminal sites on the Atlantic coast. The Passamaquoddy area in which Eastport is located emerged as by far the least acceptable site because of the high navigational risks and the high value of the fisheries and aquatic-bird resources in the region. A study by the Department of Transport at about the same time also found the navigational dangers to be great. As a result of the conclusions reached in these studies, the Canadian government has taken the position that it cannot agree to the movement of large tankers into and out of Eastport.[65] An environmental impact study has been initiated in the United States to examine further the feasibility of building a refinery at Eastport.

Transboundary environmental concerns have frequently caused tensions among groups in areas affected by particular problems, but at the government level, relations seem to be quite amicable. Canada and the United States have consistently moved to address potential transboundary problems at an early stage, and the approach has greatly reduced the negative impact of environmental issues on bilateral relations. In addition, the IJC has been an effective mechanism for assisting in the resolution of problems. Nevertheless, environmental differences can be expected to continue to emerge because Canada and the United States have philosophies of environmental control that are based on their differing domestic situations. The United States sets specific levels for discharges from all industries and from municipal sewerage facilities wherever located, while in Canada, permissible levels vary according to the degree of pollution from other sources. This difference in standards inevitably creates difficulties in boundary areas.

---

[65] Department of External Affairs, "Communiqué," December 15, 1976.

6

Concluding Comments

The 1976-78 period has been one in which Canada-U.S. relations have benefited from improved communication between government officials of the two countries. The state of bilateral relations, however, is not a constant and can be expected to experience swings in the future as in the past. This is one important reason why a regular monitoring of Canada-U.S. relations, a monitoring both of specific trends and issues and of the overall relationship such as this report has endeavored to provide, serves a valuable function. In anticipation of the uncertainty that lies ahead, this final chapter highlights some developments in the past two years that emerge from this report and that are likely to affect the nature of the relationship in the future.

The economic constraints that the two countries face are likely to have the most immediate impact on Canada-U.S. relations. The pattern of economic growth in most Western developed countries continues to be unsatisfactory, and the outlook for the immediate future is not particularly favorable. In the past the Canadian economy has benefited considerably from the demand for imports created by any cyclical upturn or by general rapid growth in the United States. The relatively slight impact that the fairly strong economic performance of the United States in 1976 and 1977 had on Canada, however, creates some uncertainty about the extent of the economic stimulus the United States can provide to Canada. Of course, Canada's economic performance during that period was adversely affected by increases in costs that were greater than increases in productivity, a trend that is being dampened in 1978 by Canada's weak economic showing and, possibly, by the efforts of the Anti-Inflation Board. The U.S. economy, meanwhile, is affected to a much lesser extent by Canada's economic performance than vice versa. Looking ahead, investment in new energy projects is one area that can be expected to contribute to improved economic performance. The building of the Alaska Highway natural gas pipeline could stimulate the economies of both countries, and in Canada there could be much benefit from new investment in heavy-oil upgrading facilities, tar sands development, and hydro-electric projects. Once energy policy is

clarified in the United States, a number of new energy development projects will undoubtedly be initiated there.

Taking a longer-term perspective, it is possible to identify from the material covered in this report five developments that have been significant in establishing the tone of the relationship in the past two years and that may well be of even more consequence in the future.

• First, the source of needed supplies of energy has been a cause of growing concern in the United States. The United States, which has long looked to Canada for a wide assortment of resource materials, including oil and gas, both because of Canada's ample resource base and because its relative political stability makes it a secure supplier, has recently indicated it would like to expand its energy ties with Canada. It is particularly interested in new purchasing arrangements for natural gas, of which Canada recently has had excess productive capacity and the transportation of which from other than neighboring countries is complicated. The Canadian government rejects the notion of a formalized continental sharing of natural resources but has shown itself willing to sell some of its surplus production and, to some extent, to share its resources to ease regional energy shortages in the United States.

• Second, special bilateral trade arrangements continue to appear to be of interest to both countries. For example, the United States has designed its proposed tariff reductions at the MTN to be particularly beneficial to those industries — especially forest products, non-ferrous metals, and petrochemicals — for which Canada is eager to achieve better access to external markets. In turn, the United States has indicated it would like to increase its purchases of Canadian natural gas. The importance of bilateral trade for Canada rests on the fact that Canada lacks a large domestic market and is not part of a large trading bloc. Despite Canada's interest in expanding its trade with Europe and the countries bordering the Pacific Ocean, the United States continues to be by far its most important trading partner, and bilateral trade continues to be very attractive. For the United States, interest in bilateral trade has focused mainly on access to Canadian energy resources and to other raw materials for which Canada has been a traditional source of U.S. supply.

• Third, there has been a tendency for Canada to seek certain benefits for its industry as a criterion for accepting bilateral deals. For example, the "Canadian-content" issue figured very prominently in the negotiations of the Alaska Highway natural gas pipeline agreement. It has also been in the forefront of discussions regarding Canada's purchase of new jet fighters, with the various bidders offering to subcontract various amounts of the total contract to Canadian businesses. Although this kind of approach was seen in the past in defense sharing arrangements and in the creation of the auto pact, Canada's use of bilateral agreements to achieve particular domestic

economic objectives relating to industrial structure seems to have taken on renewed vigor recently.

• Fourth, the key to improved Canada-U.S. relations is not necessarily fewer or less serious bilateral problems, but better ways of defusing issues before they become serious and of handling them effectively if they do. The major actors are the Canada-U.S. experts in the U.S. executive branch and in the Canadian government, supported from time to time by the leadership at the very top. Recently the two sides have for the most part been able to exchange information early and to solve issues on their separate merits. One complicating factor in this low-key and generally successful method of solving problems, however, has been the greater interest and more active involvement of elected representatives in specific bilateral problems. This can result in a situation where the U.S. Congress and the Administration take opposing positions on the way to resolve a particular bilateral issue. Just the additional attention focused on a bilateral issue by discussion at the political level can make solving it considerably more complicated. One recent example of political actors' getting involved has been the effort in the U.S. Congress to link the solutions of the TV-advertising and convention-tax issues.

• Fifth, the sharp increase in concern over the national unity question in Canada has implications for U.S. businesses operating in Canada. The pressure for the decentralization of powers from the federal to the provincial governments goes back many years, but the pressure for action has been greatly intensified by the election of the Parti Québécois government in Quebec. While decentralization is frequently debated in terms of control over government spending, it also may affect trade within Canada. For example, federal-provincial and interprovincial difficulties could result in the creation of barriers to the free flow of goods among provinces and could also have implications at the international level by interfering with the Canadian government's commitments under international agreements such as the GATT. The potential for the provinces to act in ways that could complicate bilateral relations without Ottawa's being able effectively to do anything about it has already been in evidence in takeovers in the potash industry and the proposed takeover in the asbestos industry. If decentralization increases, foreign-owned businesses may be affected by more, and different, provincial controls. The potential for divergence between the policies of two levels of government is not restricted to Canada, however, as evidenced by serious concern about the issue of state subsidies to industry in the United States.

The improvement in Canada-U.S. relations in the past two years reflects a procedural change and not a reduction in actual and potential conflicts between the two countries. Observers of the bilateral scene sense a determined commitment by the U.S. Administration

and the Canadian government to de-escalate friction through calm negotiation. However, the increasingly loud voice of Congress in Canadian-U.S. affairs, and actions of provinces and states that may jeopardize the policies of their respective national governments, may well threaten this approach in the future. While the two national governments recognize that protectionist sentiments are very strong throughout the world and are committed to trying to withstand these pressures, they are at the same time confronted with the "buy-at-home" policies or investment incentives of junior levels of government, over which they have little control.

The challenge to the bilateral relationship in the future will be primarily economic and will stem from a combination of pressures put on both countries by changes in the world economic environment and by the actions of their own respective junior levels of government. The two national governments will have to find ways to de-escalate problems arising from both sources if the interests of Canadians and Americans are to be served.

MEMBERS OF THE CANADIAN-AMERICAN COMMITTEE

Co-Chairmen

ROBERT M. MacINTOSH
Executive Vice-President, The Bank of Nova Scotia, Toronto, Ontario

PHILIP BRIGGS
Executive Vice President, Metropolitan Life Insurance Company, New York, New York

Vice-Chairmen

STEPHEN C. EYRE
Comptroller, Citibank, N.A., New York, New York

ADAM H. ZIMMERMAN
Executive Vice President, Noranda Mines Limited, Toronto, Ontario

Members

JOHN N. ABELL
Vice President and Director, Wood Gundy Limited, Toronto, Ontario

R. L. ADAMS
Executive Vice President, Continental Oil Company, Stamford, Connecticut

J. D. ALLAN
President, The Steel Company of Canada, Limited, Toronto, Ontario

J. A. ARMSTRONG
President and Chief Executive Officer, Imperial Oil Limited, Toronto, Ontario

CHARLES F. BAIRD
President, INCO Limited, New York, New York

IAN A. BARCLAY
Chairman, British Columbia Forest Products Limited, Vancouver, B.C.

THOMAS D. BARROW
Director and Senior Vice President, Exxon Corporation, New York, New York

CARL E. BEIGIE
President and Chief Executive Officer, C. D. Howe Research Institute, Montreal, Quebec

MICHEL BÉLANGER
President and Chief Executive Officer, Provincial Bank of Canada, Montreal, Quebec

ROY F. BENNETT
President and Chief Executive Officer, Ford Motor Company of Canada, Limited, Oakville, Ontario

ROD J. BILODEAU
Chairman of the Board and Chief Executive Officer, Honeywell Limited, Scarborough, Ontario

ARDEN BURBIDGE
Burbidge Farm, Park River, North Dakota

SHIRLEY CARR
Executive Vice-President, Canadian Labour Congress, Ottawa, Ontario

W. R. CLERIHUE
Executive Vice-President — Corporate Staff, Celanese Corporation, New York, New York

HON. JOHN V. CLYNE
MacMillan Bloedel Limited, Vancouver, B.C.

THOMAS E. COVEL
Marion, Massachusetts

J. S. DEWAR
President, Union Carbide Canada Limited, Toronto, Ontario

JOHN H. DICKEY
President, Nova Scotia Pulp Limited, Halifax, Nova Scotia

JOHN S. DICKEY
President Emeritus and Bicentennial Professor of Public Affairs, Dartmouth College, Hanover, New Hampshire

THOMAS W. diZEREGA
Vice President, Northwest Pipeline Corporation, Salt Lake City, Utah

GÉRARD DOCQUIER
National Director, United Steelworkers of America, Toronto, Ontario

CLIFTON H. EATON
Group Vice-President, Gillette North America, The Gillette Company, Boston, Massachusetts

WILLIAM EBERLE
Robert Weaver Associates, Boston, Massachusetts

MARTIN EMMETT
President, International Operations, Standard Brands, Inc., New York, New York

A. J. FISHER
Chairman of the Board, Fiberglas Canada Limited, Toronto, Ontario

JOHN E. FOGARTY
President, Standard Steel, Burnham, Pennsylvania

ROBERT M. FOWLER
Chairman, Executive Committee, C. D. Howe Research Institute, Montreal, Quebec

JOHN F. GALLAGHER
Vice President, International Operations, Sears, Roebuck and Company, Chicago, Illinois

W. D. H. GARDINER
Vice Chairman, The Royal Bank of Canada, Toronto, Ontario

PAT GREATHOUSE
Vice President, International Union, UAW, Detroit, Michigan

JOHN H. HALE
Executive Vice President — Finance, Alcan Aluminium Limited, Montreal, Quebec

A. D. HAMILTON
President and Chief Executive Officer, Domtar Inc., Montreal, Quebec

JOHN A. HANNAH
Executive Director, World Food Council, New York, New York

ROBERT H. HANSEN
Senior Vice President — International, Avon Products, Inc., New York, New York

JAMES A. HENDERSON
President, American Express Company of Canada Ltd., New York, New York

ROBERT H. JONES
President, The Investors Group, Winnipeg, Manitoba

EDGAR F. KAISER, JR.
President and Chief Executive Officer, Kaiser Resources Ltd., Vancouver, B.C.

JOSEPH D. KEENAN
President of Union Label & Service Trades Department, AFL-CIO, Washington, D.C.

DONALD P. KELLY
President and Chief Executive Officer, Esmark Inc., Chicago, Illinois

DAVID KIRK
Executive Secretary, The Canadian Federation of Agriculture, Ottawa, Ontario

LANE KIRKLAND
Secretary-Treasurer, AFL-CIO, Washington, D.C.

C. CALVERT KNUDSEN
President and Chief Executive Officer, MacMillan Bloedel Limited, Vancouver, B.C.

MICHAEL M. KOERNER
President, Canada Overseas Investments Limited, Toronto, Ontario

WILLIAM J. KORSVIK
Vice-President, International Banking Department, The First National Bank of Chicago, Chicago, Illinois

J. L. KUHN
President and General Manager, 3M Canada Limited, London, Ontario

RONALD W. LANG
Director, Research and Legislation, Canadian Labour Congress, Ottawa, Ontario

HERBERT H. LANK
Honorary Director, Du Pont of Canada Limited, Montreal, Quebec

EDMOND A. LEMIEUX
Commissioner, Hydro-Québec, Montreal, Quebec

RICHARD A. LENON
Chairman and Chief Executive Officer, International Minerals and Chemical Corporation, Libertyville, Illinois

FRANKLIN A. LINDSAY
Chairman, Itek Corporation, Lexington, Massachusetts

L. K. LODGE
Chairman and President, IBM Canada Ltd., Don Mills, Ontario

DONALD S. MACDONALD
McCarthy & McCarthy, Toronto, Ontario

JULIEN MAJOR
Executive Vice President, Canadian Labour Congress, Ottawa, Ontario

PAUL M. MARSHALL
President, Brascan Resources Limited, Calgary, Alberta

FRANCIS L. MASON
Senior Vice President, The Chase Manhattan Bank, N.A., New York, New York

A. H. MASSAD
Director, Mobil Oil, and President, Exploration and Producing Division, Mobil Oil Corporation, New York, New York

DENNIS McDERMOTT
President, Canadian Labour Congress, Ottawa, Ontario

H. WALLACE MERRYMAN
Chairman and Chief Executive Officer, Avco Financial Services, Inc., Newport Beach, California

JOHN MILLER
President, National Planning Association, Washington, D.C.

DONALD R. MONTGOMERY
Secretary-Treasurer, Canadian Labour Congress, Ottawa, Ontario

HARRY E. MORGAN, JR.
Senior Vice President, Weyerhaeuser Company, Tacoma, Washington

HANS HERBERT MUNTE
Executive Vice President, International, The Continental Group, New York, New York

RICHARD W. MUZZY
Group Vice President — International, Owens-Corning Fiberglas Corporation, Toledo, Ohio

CARL E. NICKELS, JR.
Senior Vice President, Finance and Law, The Hanna Mining Company, Cleveland, Ohio

HON. VICTOR deB. OLAND
Halifax, Nova Scotia

CHARLES PERRAULT
President, Perconsult Ltd., Montreal, Quebec

RICHARD H. PETERSON
Chairman of the Board, Pacific Gas and Electric Company, San Francisco, California

C. HOYT PRICE
Director of International Studies, Gulf Oil Corporation, Pittsburgh, Pennsylvania

THOMAS A. REED
Group Vice President — International Control Systems, Honeywell Inc., Minneapolis, Minnesota

ROBERT J. RICHARDSON
Vice President — Finance, E. I. du Pont de Nemours & Co., Inc., Wilmington, Delaware

BEN L. ROUSE
Vice President — Business Machines Group, Burroughs Corporation, Detroit, Michigan

THOMAS W. RUSSELL, JR.
New York, New York

A. E. SAFARIAN
Professor, Department of Political Economy, University of Toronto, Toronto, Ontario

R. T. SAVAGE
Vice-President, Standard Oil Company of California, San Francisco, California

RICHARD J. SCHMEELK
Partner, Salomon Brothers, New York, New York

ARTHUR R. SEDER, JR.
Chairman and President, American Natural Resources Company, Detroit, Michigan

JACOB SHEINKMAN
Secretary-Treasurer, Amalgamated Clothing and Textile Workers' Union, New York, New York

R. W. SPARKS
President and Chief Executive Officer, Texaco Canada Limited, Don Mills, Ontario

W. A. STRAUSS
Chairman and Chief Executive Officer, Northern Natural Gas Company, Omaha, Nebraska

ROBERT D. STUART, JR.
Chairman, The Quaker Oats Company, Chicago, Illinois

A. McC. SUTHERLAND
Director and Senior Vice President, INCO Limited, Toronto, Ontario

DWIGHT D. TAYLOR
Senior Vice President, Crown Zellerbach Corporation, San Francisco, California

W. BRUCE THOMAS
Executive Vice President — Accounting and Finance, and Director, United States Steel Corporation, Pittsburgh, Pennsylvania

ALEXANDER C. TOMLINSON
Chairman of the Executive Committee, The First Boston Corporation, New York, New York

WILLIAM I. M. TURNER, JR.
President and Chief Executive Officer, Consolidated-Bathurst Limited, Montreal, Quebec

W. O. TWAITS
Toronto, Ontario

RICHARD H. VAUGHAN
President, Northwest Bancorporation, Minneapolis, Minnesota

A. O. WAY
Senior Vice President — Finance, General Electric Company, Fairfield, Connecticut

P. N. T. WIDDRINGTON
President and Chief Executive Officer, John Labatt Limited, London, Ontario

FRANCIS G. WINSPEAR
Edmonton, Alberta

D. MICHAEL WINTON
Chairman, Pas Lumber Company Limited, Minneapolis, Minnesota

GEORGE W. WOODS
President, TransCanada PipeLines, Toronto, Ontario

WILLIAM S. WOODSIDE
President, American Can Company, Greenwich, Connecticut

DON WOODWARD
International Trade Affairs Representative, National Association of Wheat Growers, Washington, D.C.

J. O. WRIGHT
Secretary, CCWP, Saskatchewan Wheat Pool, Regina, Saskatchewan

Honorary Members

WILLIAM DODGE
Ottawa, Ontario

CARL J. GILBERT
Dover, Massachusetts

F. PEAVEY HEFFELFINGER
Director Emeritus, Peavey Company, Minneapolis, Minnesota

HON. N. A. M. MacKENZIE
Vancouver, B.C.

M. W. MACKENZIE
Ottawa, Ontario

HAROLD SWEATT
Honorary Chairman of the Board, Honeywell Inc., Minneapolis, Minnesota

JOHN R. WHITE
New York, New York

HENRY S. WINGATE
New York, New York

DAVID J. WINTON
Minneapolis, Minnesota

SELECTED PUBLICATIONS
OF THE CANADIAN-AMERICAN COMMITTEE*

Commercial Relations

CAC-40 *Industrial Incentive Policies and Programs in the Canadian-American Context*, by John Volpe. 1976 ($2.50)

CAC-38 *A Balance of Payments Handbook*, by Caroline Pestieau. 1974 ($2.00)

CAC-32 *Toward a More Realistic Appraisal of the Automotive Agreement*, a Statement by the Committee. 1970 ($1.00)

CAC-31 *The Canada-U.S. Automotive Agreement: An Evaluation*, by Carl E. Beigie. 1970 ($3.00)

CAC-25 *A New Trade Strategy for Canada and the United States*, a Statement by the Committee. 1966 ($1.00)

Energy and Other Resources

CAC-47 *Electricity Across the Border: The Canadian-American Experience*, by Mark Perlgut. 1978 ($4.00)

CAC-45 *Safer Nuclear Power Initiatives: A Call for Canada-U.S. Action*, a Statement by the Committee. 1978 ($1.00)

CAC-44 *Uranium, Nuclear Power, and Canada-U.S. Energy Relations*, by Hugh C. McIntyre. 1978 ($4.00)

CAC-41 *Coal and Canada-U.S. Energy Relations*, by Richard L. Gordon. 1976 ($3.00)

CAC-39 *Keeping Options Open in Canada-U.S. Oil and Natural Gas Trade*, a Statement by the Committee. 1975 ($1.00)

CAC-37 *Canada, the United States, and the Third Law of the Sea Conference*, by R. M. Logan. 1974 ($3.00)

Investment

CAC-33 *Canada's Experience with Fixed and Flexible Exchange Rates in a North American Capital Market*, by Robert M. Dunn, Jr. 1971 ($2.00)

CAC-29 *The Performance of Foreign-Owned Firms in Canada*, by A. E. Safarian. 1969 ($2.00)

CAC-24 *Capital Flows Between Canada and the United States*, by Irving Brecher. 1965 ($2.00)

Other

CAC-46 *Bilateral Relations in an Uncertain World Context: Canada-U.S. Relations in 1978*, a Staff Report. 1978 ($4.00)

CAC-43 *Agriculture in an Interdependent World: U.S. and Canadian Perspectives*, by T. K. Warley. 1977 ($4.00)

CAC-42 *A Time of Difficult Transitions: Canada-U.S. Relations in 1976*, a Staff Report. 1976 ($2.00)

---

*These and other Committee publications may be ordered from the Committee's offices at 2064 Sun Life Building, Montreal, Quebec H3B 2X7, and at 1606 New Hampshire Avenue, N.W., Washington, D.C. 20009. Quantity discounts are given.

1126-39-PAM

5-08

SPONSORING ORGANIZATIONS

The C. D. Howe Research Institute is a private, non-political, non-profit organization founded in January, 1973, by the merger of the C. D. Howe Memorial Foundation and the Private Planning Association of Canada, to undertake research into Canadian economic policy issues, with emphasis on fiscal, monetary, and international trade policy.

HRI continues the activities of the PPAC. These include the work of three established committees, composed of agricultural, business, educational, labor, and professional leaders. The committees are the Canadian Economic Policy Committee, which since 1961 has been concentrating on Canadian economic issues; the Canadian-American Committee, which has dealt with relations between Canada and the United States since 1957 and is jointly sponsored by the National Planning Association in Washington and HRI; and the British-North American Committee, formed in 1969 and sponsored jointly by the British-North American Research Association in London, the National Planning Association, and HRI. Each of the three committees meets twice a year to consider important current issues and to sponsor and review studies that contribute to a better public understanding of such issues.

In addition to taking over the publications of the three PPAC committees, HRI releases the work of its staff, and occasionally of outside authors, in four other publications: *HRI Observations*, six or seven of which are published each year; *Policy Review and Outlook*, published annually; *Special Studies*, to provide detailed analysis of major policy issues; and *Commentaries*, to give wide circulation to the views of experts on issues of current Canadian interest.

HRI publications, including those of the Canadian-American Committee, are available from the Institute's offices, 2064 Sun Life Building, Montreal, Quebec H3B 2X7 (Tel. 514-879-1254).

The National Planning Association is an independent, private, non-profit, non-political organization that carries on research and policy formulation in the public interest. NPA was founded during the Great Depression of the 1930s, when conflicts among the major economic groups — business, farmers, and labor — threatened to paralyze national decision-making on the critical issues confronting American society. It was dedicated, in the words of its statement of purpose, to the task "of getting [these] diverse groups to work together . . . [and] to provide on specific problems concrete programs for action planned in the best traditions of a functioning democracy." Such democratic planning, NPA believes, involves the development of effective governmental and private policies and programs not only by official agencies but also through the independent initiative and cooperation of the main private-sector groups concerned. To preserve and strengthen American political and economic democracy, therefore, the necessary government actions have to be consistent with, and supportive of, a dynamic private sector.

NPA brings together influential and knowledgeable leaders from business, labor, agriculture, and the applied and academic professions to serve on policy committees, one of which is the Canadian-American Committee. These committees identify emerging problems confronting the nation at home and abroad and seek to develop and agree upon policies and programs for coping with them. The research and writing for these committees are provided by NPA's professional staff and, as required, by outside experts.

In addition, NPA's professional staff undertakes research designed to provide data and ideas for policy-makers and -planners in government and the private sector. This research includes the preparation on a regular basis of economic and demographic projections for the national economy, regions, states, and metropolitan areas; the development of program planning and evaluation techniques; research on national goals and priorities; analyses of welfare and dependency problems, employment and manpower needs, education, medical care, environmental protection, energy, and other economic and social issues confronting American society; and studies of changing international realities and their implications for U.S. policies.

NPA publications, including those of the Canadian-American Committee, can be obtained from the Association's offices, 1606 New Hampshire Avenue, N.W., Washington, D.C. 20009 (Tel. 202-265-7685).

CAC 46/$4.00
NPA 165